RESILIENT TRADE THEORY

Sovereign Security in an Age of Interdependence

KENNETH TUTTLE WILHELM

notionpress.com

INDIA • SINGAPORE • MALAYSIA

ISBN
Paperback 979-8-90136-601-1
Hardcase 979-8-90362-855-1

CONTENTS

Preface *5*

Introduction - Why Resilient Trade Theory, and Why Now *13*

Part I Foundations of Resilient Trade Theory **25**

Chapter 1 Why Resilience, Why Now 27

Chapter 2 Defining Resilience in the Economic Sphere 39

Chapter 3 Ethics, Sovereignty, and the Moral Imperative 52

Part II The Structure of Resilient Trade Theory **65**

Chapter 4 The Strategic Categorisation of Goods and Sectors 67

Chapter 5 The Economics of Strategic Capacity 82

Chapter 6 Labour Systems as a Core Resilience Asset 97

Chapter 7 Institutional Design for Resilience Governance 112

Part III The Resilient Trade Model in Practice 127

Chapter 8 Domestic Capacity Building 129

Chapter 9 Differentiated Trade Policy 146

Chapter 10 Social Cohesion as Economic Infrastructure 162

Chapter 11 Diplomacy and Global Resilience Alliances 179

Part IV Critiques, Extensions, and Global Applications 193

Chapter 12 Common Critiques and Misconceptions 195

Chapter 13 Regional Application Models 208

Chapter 14 Resilience in a Polycrisis World 226

Part V Conclusion 245

Chapter 15 Resilience as a Strategic Virtue 247

Author's Concluding Remarks *263*

About the Author *267*

PREFACE

I was born into a world already on fire.

Some of my earliest memories are not of playgrounds or schoolyards, but of television images from the Vietnam War - grainy footage, maps, an endless commentary about battles and withdrawals. I didn't understand the details, but I understood enough: grown-ups were worried, the world could break, and decisions made far away could change the course of ordinary lives.

Since then, I have lived through more cycles of crisis than I can easily count. Oil shocks. Recessions. Currency collapses. The end of the Cold War, which briefly felt like a clearing of the air. The slow return of geopolitical rivalry. Regional conflicts that never quite stayed "regional." The global financial crisis. COVID-19. Wars that rearranged energy systems and food flows in a matter of months.

Each time, I watched the same pattern repeat with small variations:

- political turmoil or conflict.
- economic disruption.
- and then, often with a lag, social strain as people struggled to absorb the shock.

Trade was always there in the background, sometimes as a lifeline, sometimes as a channel of contagion, sometimes as a lever of pressure. Over the last few decades, as global integration deepened, that background role has moved steadily to the foreground. Supply chains extended. Production clustered. Critical inputs concentrated in a small number of places and firms. The gains were real: cheaper goods, rapid innovation, new opportunities for developing economies.

But each crisis also revealed something else: the more tightly we wove our economic systems together, the more exposed we became when something snapped.

I have never been a romantic about autarky. I don't believe in a world of walled-off economies or nostalgia for some imagined self-sufficient past. Trade has lifted standards of living and connected societies in ways earlier generations could only dream of. Yet it has also created new forms of dependency, some benign, some profoundly dangerous.

What troubled me, and still troubles me, is how casually we often accept those dangerous dependencies. How easily we normalise the idea that a country might not be able to feed itself in a crisis, or access basic medicines, or power its grid, or keep its digital infrastructure running without the permission, explicit or implicit, of others who may not share its values or interests.

Resilient Trade Theory grew out of that discomfort.

This book is my attempt to give words and structure to a question that has been with me, in one form or another, since childhood:

What can countries and regions do to protect themselves, economically and politically, without betraying the values they claim to stand for, and without walking away from the world?

I am a child of war, but I am also a witness to peace, cooperation, and the extraordinary potential of open exchange. I do not want a future defined only by defensive reflexes and hardened borders. At the same time, I cannot ignore the reality that repeated shocks, weaponised interdependence, and climate disruption have altered the basic risk landscape.

The old promise, "more trade will fix this", is no longer enough.

This book exists to explore what comes next.

What This Book Tries To Do

Resilient Trade Theory is not a manifesto for isolation, and it is not an argument for protectionism dressed up in new language. It is, instead, an attempt to:

- distinguish clearly between **what we must protect** and **what we can freely trade**
- take seriously the idea that some capacities, food, basic medicine, core energy, digital and logistical backbones, are not optional in a crisis
- show how a country or bloc might build strategic resilience in those essentials while remaining open, innovative, and engaged in non-essential sectors
- and place all of this within a moral frame that takes sovereignty, dignity, and justice seriously

The book has two main pillars:

- **Resilient Trade Theory** - the conceptual foundation: why resilience matters, how it relates to ethics and sovereignty, and why we need to treat certain sectors differently from others.

- **The Resilient Trade Model** - the practical architecture: how to classify sectors, build domestic and allied capacity, design differentiated trade policies, support essential workers, create governance structures, and engage in diplomacy that strengthens resilience rather than eroding it.

You will find, throughout, a tension that I have no interest in smoothing over: the tension between openness and safety, efficiency and redundancy, global integration and national autonomy. I don't believe that tension can be resolved once and for all. But I do believe we can handle it with more honesty and more discipline than we have so far.

Why I Wrote It This Way

I have chosen not to write this as a dense, technical economics text. There is no shortage of excellent formal work on trade, comparative advantage, and global value chains. That work matters, and this book does not try to replace it.

My aim here is different. I want to speak directly to:

- policy professionals trying to make sense of repeated crises
- think-tank analysts and researchers wrestling with "resilience" as more than a slogan
- graduate students and scholars searching for a bridge between conventional trade theory and the lived reality of economic coercion, climate shocks, and systemic risk
- and practitioners who see, every day, how abstract decisions ripple through food systems, energy networks, and local communities

I have written in plain language, as much as possible, while respecting the complexity of the subject. Where I draw on academic and policy work, I use light endnotes so the main argument remains readable. Where I make normative claims, I try to say so plainly.

I have also tried to keep faith with lived experience, the sense, shared by many, that the current arrangement feels *too fragile*. Not in a dramatic, headline-grabbing way, but in the quiet recognition that it doesn't take much anymore to push systems to the edge.

What You Can Expect

If you read this book from beginning to end, you will move through five arcs:

1. **Foundations** - how the old "efficiency-first" trade story came undone, and what resilience means when we put it at the centre.
2. **Structure** - how to think systematically about essential and non-essential sectors, strategic capacity, labour, and governance.
3. **Practice** - how those ideas translate into domestic policy, trade design, social cohesion, and diplomacy.
4. **Critique and application** - where RTT is vulnerable to misuse, where it must answer tough questions, and how fragments of it already exist in the European Union, East Asia, the Gulf, Latin America, and the Global South.
5. **Future** - how resilience operates in a "polycrisis" world of climate disruption, AI risk, and demographic shifts, and why I believe resilience itself should be treated as a strategic virtue.

I don't expect you to agree with every step. In fact, if you are trained in orthodox economics, international relations, or security studies, you will likely find parts you want to push back on. Good. This book is not meant to close the debate; it is meant to give that debate clearer contours.

What I hope is that, by the time you finish, you will:

- be slower to accept dangerous forms of dependency as "just how the world works"
- be more willing to ask which sectors are truly essential, and which are not
- see labour systems and social cohesion as core components of economic resilience, not side issues
- and have a more concrete sense of how trade policy, industrial policy, and diplomacy might be redesigned to match the world we actually live in, rather than the one we thought we had

An Invitation

In the end, this book is an invitation to a conversation that needs to widen: across ministries, across disciplines, and across borders.

I am a child of the Vietnam War era, but I am writing for a generation that will face its own storms -some already visible, others still forming. They will not have the luxury of assuming that systems built for a different age will hold under new pressures.

If *Resilient Trade Theory* helps you, in your own work, to think a little more clearly about what must be protected, what can be shared, and how to do both without losing sight of your values, then it will have served its purpose.

The chapters that follow are my contribution to that effort. The real work will be yours.

– Kenneth Tuttle Wilhelm, 2022–2025

In December of 2022, Janet Yellen, former US Secretary of the Treasury, penned an online article for Project Syndicate. The title of this article was "Resilient Trade."

This was the starting point that motivated me to develop this book.

– KTW

INTRODUCTION - WHY RESILIENT TRADE THEORY, AND WHY NOW

At the beginning of the 21st century, a simple story guided much of economic policy: liberalise trade, integrate markets, and the rest would follow. Growth would accelerate, shocks would be softened by diversified supply, and peace would be reinforced by mutual dependence.

For several decades, this story seemed to hold. Trade expanded faster than global GDP. Supply chains stretched across continents. Governments built development strategies around export-led growth and participation in global value chains. The "efficiency-first" model became conventional wisdom.[1]

Then the edges began to fray.

The global financial crisis revealed how tightly coupled and brittle key systems had become. COVID-19 exposed just how quickly supply chains for basic medical goods, food, and electronics could seize when multiple regions shut down at once. Extreme weather events now routinely close ports, damage infrastructure, and undermine harvests. Geopolitical tensions have brought export bans, sanctions, and technology controls squarely into the realm of trade policy.

The World Trade Organization's own flagship report on "economic resilience and trade" now acknowledges that the same interdependence that spreads opportunity can also transmit disruption, and that the trading system is simultaneously **more vulnerable and more resilient** than we once assumed.[2] The World Economic Forum's Global Risks Reports speak openly of a "polycrisis" era: overlapping shocks in energy, food, climate, security, and technology that interact and amplify one another.[3]

In this environment, the old promise - that openness and efficiency alone would deliver stability and prosperity - no longer looks sufficient. It is not that trade has failed. It is that we demanded more from one idea than it was ever designed to bear.

This book is written into that gap.

What This Book Argues

At its core, *Resilient Trade Theory* makes three claims.

First, resilience in essentials is not a luxury. It is a *duty*. Governments are not only responsible for growth and competitiveness; they are responsible for ensuring that people can eat, access basic medicine, keep the lights on, communicate, and exercise political agency even when the world around them becomes unstable. That duty cannot be outsourced entirely to markets or foreign providers.

Second, resilience does not require isolation. The choice is not between full global integration and autarky. There is a middle path: **intentional interdependence**. Countries and economic blocs can remain deeply engaged with the world, while deliberately shaping which dependencies they accept, which they share with partners, and which they refuse.

Third, trade is not value-neutral. Beneath the language of prices and flows lie questions of power, justice, and vulnerability. Who controls critical chokepoints? Who bears the brunt when systems fail? Who can be coerced - and by whom? A serious trade doctrine has to look those questions in the eye, not treat them as unfortunate side effects.

To respond to these realities, I propose a framework with two tightly connected parts:

- **Resilient Trade Theory (RTT)** - the "why": a normative and strategic account of why countries and blocs should distinguish between *essential* and *non-essential* goods, and why a certain level of domestic and allied capacity in essentials is ethically and strategically required.
- **The Resilient Trade Model** - the "how": a practical architecture for implementing RTT, covering sector classification, domestic capacity building, labour systems, governance, differentiated trade policy, and resilience-oriented diplomacy.

Together, they suggest a different headline for trade in the 21st century:

Not *peace through trade* at any cost, but *strength through balance* - a deliberate balance between openness and autonomy, efficiency and redundancy, growth and continuity.

Who This Book Is For

This is not a technical economics text in the narrow sense. You will not find formal models or dense equations here. That work is valuable - and I hope future researchers will build the mathematical backbone that RTT would need for full integration into mainstream trade theory - but it is not the purpose of this volume.

Instead, this book is written for:

- **Policy professionals** in ministries of trade, economy, defence, agriculture, energy, and foreign affairs grappling with how to adjust policy to a world of repeated shocks.
- **Think-tank researchers and analysts** working at the intersection of economics, security, and governance, who need an organising framework for often disconnected debates.
- **Graduate students and faculty** in political science, international relations, public policy, and economics, looking for a conceptual bridge between orthodox trade theory and the emerging literature on resilience, strategic autonomy, and geo-economics.
- **Practitioners in international organisations**, regional blocs, and development institutions who are trying to support resilience without closing off opportunity - especially in the Global South.

The examples and vignettes draw from East Asia (including Taiwan, Japan, South Korea, the United States, and Pacific island states), Southeast Asia, Europe, and the Americas. Sectorally, I focus on agriculture, energy, research and development, technology, and military integration/readiness - because these are where resilience questions become unavoidable.

The book uses light endnotes rather than heavy in-text citation, to keep the argument readable while still pointing to sources and debates for those who want to go deeper.

What This Book Does – and Does Not – Try to Do

It may help to be clear about scope.

This book **does not** attempt to:

- offer a complete formal model of resilient trade
- provide a universal policy checklist that any country can apply without adaptation
- predict specific geopolitical outcomes or future crises

What it **does** aim to do is:

- articulate a coherent *theory* of why resilience in trade matters, grounded in ethics, sovereignty, and social cohesion
- propose a *model* - an institutional and policy architecture - for how that theory could be implemented in practice
- show how elements of RTT already exist, partially and imperfectly, in real regional and national strategies
- engage directly with critiques from both political and orthodox economic perspectives
- and, perhaps most importantly, give policymakers and scholars a **language** for thinking about trade and resilience together, rather than in parallel conversations

If this book succeeds, it will not be because everyone agrees with its conclusions. It will be because the discussion about trade, security, and justice becomes more honest, more structured, and less anchored to assumptions that no longer fit the world we inhabit.

How the Book Is Structured

The book is organised into five parts. Each part builds on the last, but they can also be read selectively depending on your interests.

PART I - FOUNDATIONS OF RESILIENT TRADE THEORY

Chapter 1 - The Global Trade Assumption That Broke

We begin with the promise and fragility of the neoliberal trade orthodoxy. The chapter traces how "efficiency-first" globalisation came to dominate thinking, why it worked for a time, and how successive crises - financial, epidemiological, geopolitical, and climatic - have exposed its structural vulnerabilities. It closes by making the case that *resilience*, not *raw efficiency*, must now become the guiding principle for trade policy.[2] [4]

Chapter 2 - Defining Resilience in the Economic Sphere

"Resilience" is a fashionable word. It is also maddeningly vague. This chapter disaggregates the concept into economic, social, and geopolitical dimensions. It distinguishes resilience from autarky and redundancy, and clarifies the difference between *strategic autonomy* and *absolute self-sufficiency*. We look at case studies of both failed and successful resilience attempts - from brittle just-in-time systems to societies that have built deep buffers without withdrawing from the world.

Chapter 3 - Ethics, Sovereignty, and the Moral Imperative

Here the argument moves from strategy to obligation. If citizens entrust governments with their safety and continuity, what does that imply for trade and economic design? Drawing on work in political philosophy and human security, the chapter argues that securing essential capacities is not merely smart policy; it is a moral duty owed across class, region, and generation.[5] It introduces the idea of "continuity justice": ensuring that today's gains do not come at the cost of tomorrow's basic security.

PART II - THE STRUCTURE OF RESILIENT TRADE THEORY

Chapter 4 - The Strategic Categorisation of Goods and Sectors

Not all vulnerabilities are equal. This chapter sets out a structured way to classify sectors and goods into tiers: lifeline essentials, enabling infrastructure, important but non-critical sectors, and discretionary goods. It explains criteria for classification, how to handle "grey zones", and why the classification has to be dynamic as technologies and geopolitics evolve. We also explore vulnerability mapping and stress-testing of interdependence.

Chapter 5 - The Economics of Strategic Capacity

Here we revisit comparative advantage through a resilience lens. What does it mean to accept higher unit costs in essentials in exchange for lower systemic risk? How do we think about "strategic sufficiency" versus market-led efficiency? We look at investment logic that favours continuity and option value over short-term returns, and at how these ideas sit alongside orthodox trade and industrial policy thinking.[2] [6]

Chapter 6 - Labour Systems as a Core Resilience Asset

Resilience is not only built from machines and stockpiles; it is built from people. This chapter treats labour systems - wages, training, regional distribution, and voice - as infrastructure. It argues for a minimum liveable wage in essential sectors, for workforce development programmes tied to strategic objectives, and for using resilience investments to support regional rebalancing rather than deepen divides.

Chapter 7 - Institutional Design for Resilience Governance

Theory without institutions is wishful thinking. This chapter introduces the idea of a **Resilient Trade Authority (RTA)** - or equivalent - as a central node for classification, audits, simulations, and cross-ministerial coordination. We examine how to insulate such bodies from short-term politics while keeping them democratically accountable, and how to embed transparency, learning, and adaptive governance into their mandates.

PART III - THE RESILIENT TRADE MODEL IN PRACTICE

Chapter 8 - Domestic Capacity Building

This chapter moves from theory to implementation. It looks at how public investment, incentives, and regulation can be used to build and maintain capacity in essential sectors - from agriculture and energy to pharmaceuticals and secure digital infrastructure. We explore strategic reserves, decentralised production, and the alignment of education policy with resilience goals.

Chapter 9 - Differentiated Trade Policy

Here we tackle trade instruments head on. The chapter outlines a tiered approach: selective protection and friend-shoring in essentials; openness in non-essentials; and resilience clauses in trade agreements. We discuss tools such as import licensing, tariffs, content rules, and alliance-based sourcing - and the safeguards needed to prevent these from drifting into broad protectionism.

Chapter 10 - Social Cohesion as Economic Infrastructure

Resilience built on social fragmentation is an illusion. This chapter examines how cooperative ownership, small and medium enterprise (SME) development, and community wealth-building can make resilience *visible* in daily life. It also considers inclusive planning processes as a way to deepen legitimacy and reduce the risk that resilience policies are perceived as top-down impositions.

Chapter 11 - Diplomacy and Global Resilience Alliances

National resilience exists within a global system. This chapter explores how RTT translates into diplomacy: resilience blocs, friend-shoring corridors, and multilateral pacts on shared threats such as pandemics, climate, and cyber risk. We examine both the promise and the dangers - fragmentation, club dynamics, and new forms of dependency - and argue for a cooperative resilience order rooted in principle as well as price.

PART IV - CRITIQUES, EXTENSIONS, AND GLOBAL APPLICATIONS

Chapter 12 - Common Critiques and Misconceptions

A serious framework must be able to withstand criticism. This chapter engages directly with three families of critique: that RTT is simply protectionism in disguise; that it leads inexorably to isolation and blocs; and that it conflicts with orthodox principles of efficiency and innovation. We separate valid warnings from caricatures and identify where RTT itself must be self-limiting.

Chapter 13 - Regional Application Models

Here we look at how elements of RTT are already visible, if unevenly, in real-world strategies: the EU's pursuit of "open strategic autonomy"; Taiwan's semiconductor-anchored resilience; Finland's institutionalised preparedness; the UAE's food security strategy; Vietnam's adaptive integration in global value chains; Brazil's food and fuel redundancy; and quieter "silent resilience" practices in parts of the Global South. The goal is not to elevate any one model, but to distil lessons and cautions.

Chapter 14 - Resilience in a Polycrisis World

This chapter places RTT explicitly within the polycrisis frame. It explores how climate disruption, AI risk, and demographic shifts change the resilience calculus and push RTT from a static blueprint to an evolving doctrine. We examine climate-resilient capacity, AI as both tool and systemic risk, ageing and youthful societies, and the need for continuous doctrinal adaptation rather than one-off reforms.[3] [7]

PART V - CONCLUSION

Chapter 15 - Resilience as a Strategic Virtue

The final chapter steps back to reflect on Resilient Trade Theory as a choice about who we want to be under pressure. It revisits the shift from "peace through trade" to "strength through balance", suggests new ways of measuring success beyond GDP and export volumes, and lays out what the future demands from trade, policy, and leadership. The chapter closes with a simple test: when the next storm arrives - and it will - will our people still have food, power, medicine, trustworthy information, and the freedom to act without external blackmail?

How to Read This Book

You do not need to read this book in one straight line. Different readers may want to approach it differently:

- If you are interested in the *philosophical and normative* arguments, Part I and Chapter 15 will be most relevant.

- If you are working on *policy design or institutional reform*, Parts II and III provide a structured toolkit.
- If your focus is on *regional or global implications*, Part IV is the place to start.

A Final Word Before We Begin

This book is written with a certain conviction, but not with the illusion of finality. Resilient Trade Theory is offered as a compass, not a map. The world it describes is changing quickly, and no single framework will fit all times and places.

But the underlying question is not going away:

What must we be able to secure, together and on our own, if we want our societies to remain free, dignified, and capable of governing themselves in the storms to come?

If this book helps you think more clearly about that question, whether you agree with its answers or not, it will have done its work.

Endnotes

1. Rodrik, D. (2011). *The Globalization Paradox: Democracy and the Future of the World Economy*. W. W. Norton.
2. World Trade Organization. (2021). *World Trade Report 2021: Economic resilience and trade*. WTO.
3. World Economic Forum. (2023). *Global Risks Report 2023*; see also commentary on the emerging "polycrisis" frame.
4. IISD. (2021). *Increased Trade Cooperation Would Build Economic Resilience, WTO Says*. International Institute for Sustainable Development, summarising WTR 2021 findings.

5. UNDP. (2023). *New Threats to Human Security in the Anthropocene: Demanding greater solidarity*. United Nations Development Programme.
6. Aiginger, K., & Rodrik, D. (2020). Rebirth of industrial policy and an agenda for the twenty-first century. *Journal of Industry, Competition and Trade, 20*(2), 189–207.
7. Lawrence, M., Janzwood, S., & Homer-Dixon, T. (2024). Global polycrisis: The causal mechanisms of crisis entanglement. *Global Sustainability, 7*, e10.

PART I

Foundations of Resilient Trade Theory

CHAPTER 1

WHY RESILIENCE, WHY NOW

The late twentieth and early twenty-first century were shaped by a powerful belief: if states opened their markets, deepened trade, and pursued efficiency above all, peace and prosperity would follow. This belief informed trade agreements, industrial strategies, and corporate decisions across regions and sectors. It encouraged long supply chains, lean inventories, and dependence on the lowest-cost producer, wherever that producer happened to be.

For a time, this seemed to work. Yet over the last decade, a series of overlapping shocks has made the limits of that assumption visible. A pandemic disrupted medical supply chains. Wars and sanctions spilled over into energy markets and food systems. Climate extremes halted river traffic and damaged infrastructure. Cyberattacks hit pipelines, ports, hospitals, and logistics networks. Export controls were used as strategic tools, and access to critical inputs became a lever of pressure rather than a neutral fact of commerce.[1]

What these events revealed was not that trade is undesirable, but that an economic architecture built entirely around efficiency is structurally fragile. Systems that function brilliantly in calm conditions can fail quickly when exposed to correlated shocks and deliberate coercion. The question facing policymakers, scholars, and institutions is no longer whether trade is useful. The question is how trade should be structured so that societies remain able to feed, power, heal, and defend themselves when conditions deteriorate.

Resilient Trade Theory (RTT) is a response to that question. It does not call for isolation. It does not ask countries to reject globalisation or abandon cooperation. Instead, it proposes a more deliberate form of openness, one that distinguishes clearly between essential and non-essential sectors, and that aligns trade, industrial policy, labour systems, and diplomacy with that distinction. Its aim is simple: to enable countries and economic blocs to remain engaged with the world, while retaining the ability to stand on their own feet when it matters most.

1. From Efficiency-First to Strength Through Balance

The dominant trade paradigm of recent decades can be summarised as "efficiency-first." The central goal was to minimise unit cost. Production was located where labour or energy was cheapest, inventories were cut back, and just-in-time delivery became a norm. Comparative advantage was interpreted in increasingly narrow terms, with price taken as the primary signal.

This approach produced clear gains in many areas: lower consumer prices, increased product variety, and rapid diffusion of technologies. But it also had costs that were neither well measured nor well governed. As supply chains stretched and specialised, they became more exposed to local disruption. As key inputs were concentrated in a few locations, entire systems began to depend on single points of failure. As trade intensity increased, so did the ability of states to use trade networks as instruments of pressure.[2]

RTT does not dismiss efficiency. It argues that efficiency alone is no longer a sufficient organising principle. In a world of higher volatility and visible coercion, **continuity in essential sectors** must be treated as a public good. This requires a rebalancing of priorities:

- **Efficiency remains desirable**, especially in non-essential sectors.
- **Resilience becomes non-negotiable** in sectors where failure would cascade across society.
- **Openness is differentiated** according to strategic importance and risk, rather than applied uniformly.

The core idea is "strength through balance." Countries should remain open where openness is safe, deepen allied interdependence where it is essential, and introduce targeted protections only where continuity truly demands it. This is neither nostalgia for self-sufficiency nor nostalgia for frictionless globalisation. It is an attempt to bring trade policy into alignment with the risk structure of the present.

2. Four Structural Shifts in the Risk Landscape

The case for RTT arises from structural change rather than short-term disturbance. Four shifts are particularly important.

Geoeconomic Coercion

Global production networks and payment systems now give states the ability to exert pressure not only through tariffs but through export bans, extraterritorial sanctions, standards restrictions, and targeted denial of critical inputs. The same networks that once seemed to guarantee mutual interest can be used to shape or constrain another state's choices.[3]

Climate Disruption

Climate change has moved from a distant concern to an immediate operational reality. Heat waves limit physical labour and strain grids. Droughts reduce river levels and disrupt barge traffic. Storms and floods damage ports, rail links, and warehouses. Wildfires and smoke affect air quality and reduce transport and logistics capacity. These events are no longer rare. They recur, and they interact with one another.[4]

Digital and Cyber Fragility

Essential sectors depend on digital control systems and data flows. Grid operations, ports, water treatment plants, and hospital supply chains are all mediated by software. This creates efficiency, but it also creates an expanded attack surface. Ransomware incidents, supply-chain malware, and targeted attacks on industrial control systems have already demonstrated how quickly digital disruptions can translate into physical and social crises.

Demographic and Labour Strain

In many advanced economies, key technical workforces are aging faster than they are being replaced. Skilled trades in maintenance, utilities, food systems, and manufacturing are often in short supply. At the same time, political constraints limit large-scale labour mobility. This combination makes it harder to sustain and expand the human capacity that resilience requires.

Taken together, these shifts increase the probability, frequency, and correlation of shocks. They change not only the expected value of trade relationships, but the distribution of risks around them. RTT is one attempt to adjust policy to this new distribution.

3. What Resilient Trade Theory Is—and Is Not

To avoid confusion, it is important to define the scope of RTT clearly.

RTT is

- A way to **classify sectors** by strategic importance, separating those that are essential for survival and governance from those that are not.
- A framework for **building domestic and allied capacity** in essential sectors, including stockpiles, localised production of chokepoint goods, resilient logistics, and skilled labour.
- A guide for **differentiated trade policy**, keeping non-essential sectors open while applying calibrated safeguards and allied sourcing in essentials.
- A recognition that **labour equity is a resilience input**, minimum liveable wages and credible training pathways in essential sectors are part of system stability, not purely social policy.
- A call for **institutional design**, including independent bodies charged with resilience audits, scenario exercises, public reporting, and sunset reviews.
- A basis for **resilience-oriented diplomacy**, where trade agreements include continuity obligations, emergency procedures, and mechanisms for joint preparedness.

RTT is not

- A justification for generalized tariffs or permanent protection.
- A call for complete self-sufficiency or isolation from global markets.
- A rejection of comparative advantage or innovation.

- A doctrine that seeks to freeze structures in place. It assumes that technologies, alliances, and vulnerabilities will change, and that policy must be able to change with them.

Key Working Definitions

- **Essential sectors:** Goods and services whose interruption would rapidly undermine health, safety, governance, or territorial security (food and agriculture inputs, power and grid equipment, pharmaceuticals and medical supplies, water treatment, core digital infrastructure, and key defence-related materials).
- **Non-essential sectors:** Goods and services whose interruption, while economically significant, does not immediately compromise basic functioning (most consumer goods, luxury products, entertainment, many services).
- **Strategic sufficiency**: The minimum level of domestic and allied capability required to ensure that, under plausible shocks, a country can maintain essential flows until alternative arrangements can be brought online.

The central claim is that essential and non-essential sectors should not be governed by identical rules. They do not carry the same consequences when they fail. They should not be treated as if they do.

4. A Comparative View: Three Trade Logics

A useful way to understand RTT is to set it alongside the two dominant alternatives: efficiency-first globalisation and autarkic self-sufficiency.

Exhibit 1 - Three Trade Logics Compared

Approach	Core objective	Advantages	Main risks
Efficiency-first	Minimise unit cost and maximise aggregate output	Lower prices, increased variety, diffusion of technology	High exposure to shocks; concentration in critical inputs; vulnerability to coercion
Autarky	Maximise self-sufficiency in most sectors	Reduced exposure to foreign shocks; control over standards and production	High fiscal and welfare costs; slower innovation; risk of stagnation or authoritarian drift
Resilient Trade (RTT)	Ensure continuity in essentials while preserving openness in non-essentials	Balance between security and innovation; targeted redundancy; cooperative resilience with allies	Requires capable institutions, political discipline, and sustained public communication

RTT does not claim to eliminate risk. No economic system can do that. Its objective is to reduce systemic vulnerability in the sectors where failure would be most damaging, without sacrificing the benefits of openness where those benefits are highest and the risks are manageable.

5. Vignette: Low Water on a Strategic River

Consider a European river that serves as a major artery for barge traffic. In a particularly dry summer, water levels drop to historic lows. Barges that normally carry grain, fertilizers, chemicals, and heavy components for energy infrastructure are forced to operate at reduced capacity or halt altogether. Rail lines and highways, already busy, struggle to absorb the redirected volume. Storage facilities near the river begin to fill; plants downstream start to worry about feedstock shortages.

If the system has been designed purely around efficiency, there may be few alternatives ready. Diversion plans are improvised. Transport prices spike. Some factories curtail production. A number of utilities delay maintenance because critical parts cannot be delivered on time.

If, instead, the river has been treated as a vulnerability within a broader resilience framework, the picture looks different. Inland depots have been built along alternative corridors. Strategic reserves of key inputs are held away from the most exposed locations. Pre-negotiated protocols shift volumes automatically onto rail and road when water levels fall below a certain trigger. Corridors have been tested in joint exercises. The outage is still inconvenient. But it does not become a national emergency.

This is not an abstract scenario. Events of this type have already occurred.[5] The question is whether they remain one-off crises, or whether countries treat them as signals to redesign systems before more severe shocks arrive.

6. Why This Matters for Policy and Scholarship

For **policy institutions and think-tanks**, RTT offers a more granular framework for analysis. Debates that might previously have been conducted in terms of "pro-trade" and "anti-trade" can instead be organised around specific sectors, defined vulnerabilities, and explicit thresholds. It becomes possible to ask: which inputs must we be able to secure under stress, and by what combination of domestic production, allied sourcing, and reserves?

For **political science**, RTT opens a path between two existing strands of work. It connects research on interdependence and coercion with research on state capacity, legitimacy, and regime resilience. It suggests that how a state structures its essential sectors has direct implications for its foreign policy autonomy and its internal political stability.[6]

For **economics**, RTT is an invitation rather than a closure. It does not discard comparative advantage, but it suggests that the concept should be re-examined in the presence of disruption externalities, option value of critical capacity, and endogenous coercion risk. The task for formal work is to incorporate those elements in ways that remain tractable but better match the real environment.[7]

For **students and practitioners**, RTT provides language and tools that can be used immediately: sector classification, essentiality registers, allied corridors, continuity clauses, and resilience audits. It allows discussions of resilience to move from general aspiration to concrete design.

7. A Practical Entry Point: Five Questions for the First Year

A country or bloc that wishes to begin applying RTT does not need to solve every problem at once. It can start by answering a small set of foundational questions.

1. **Which sectors are essential?**

   Produce an initial list of essential sectors and critical inputs, with short dossiers describing current dependence, key suppliers, and plausible disruption scenarios.

2. **Where are the main chokepoints?**

   Identify the most significant single points of failure in each essential sector, ports, factories, IT systems, geographic bottlenecks, and assess how long it would take to recover if each failed.

3. **What is the current workforce position in essentials?**

   Map vacancy rates, age profiles, and training pipelines in agriculture, energy systems, medical production, water infrastructure, logistics, and defence-related industries.

4. **Which allies are structural, not merely rhetorical?**

   Determine which partners have the capacity, reliability, and political alignment to be part of trusted supply corridors, and begin discussing continuity obligations and emergency procedures.

5. **Who will own the resilience portfolio?**

   Decide which institution, existing or new, will be responsible for resilience audits, joint simulations, public reporting, and recommending the activation or sunset of specific measures.

Toolkit 1 - A Short Briefing Note for Senior Officials

- **Objective:** Guarantee continuity in essential sectors while preserving openness and innovation elsewhere.
- **Method:** Classify sectors, strengthen domestic and allied capacity in essentials, and embed continuity mechanisms into trade, procurement, and labour policy.

- **Guardrails:** Use independent audits, clear thresholds, and sunset provisions to prevent drift into generalized protectionism.
- **Communication:** Explain to the public that modest resilience investments in essentials are a form of insurance against severe disruptions, not a rejection of trade.
- **First step:** Commit to an essential sector register and a baseline resilience audit within twelve months.

8. Scope and Direction of This Book

This book is intended as an introduction rather than a final word. It does not attempt to supply a complete mathematical treatment of resilience in trade. That work is important, and it will need to be done. Here, the purpose is different: to provide an integrated conceptual framework and a set of practical tools that policymakers, researchers, and students can use to think more clearly about the problem.

Subsequent chapters will:

- Define resilience in greater detail and distinguish it from autarky and redundancy.
- Develop the ethical and sovereign arguments for securing essential sectors.
- Describe the institutional arrangements needed to govern resilient trade.
- Explore differentiated trade policy, labour systems, social cohesion, and international alliances in more depth.
- Offer regional and sectoral examples from East Asia, North America, Europe, Southeast Asia, and Latin America.

The underlying conviction is straightforward. In an era of overlapping crises and visible coercion, resilience in essential sectors is not a luxury. It is part of the minimum architecture of a responsible state. Trade will remain vital. The question is no longer whether we trade, but how we trade while ensuring that our societies can endure.

Endnotes

1. Farrell, H., & Newman, A. L. (2019). Weaponized interdependence: How global economic networks shape state coercion. *International Security, 44*(1), 42–79.
2. WTO. (2021). *World Trade Report 2021: Economic resilience and trade.* World Trade Organization.
3. IMF. (2023). *Geoeconomic fragmentation and the future of multilateralism.* International Monetary Fund.
4. IPCC. (2023). *AR6 Synthesis Report: Climate Change 2023.* Intergovernmental Panel on Climate Change.
5. OECD. (2021). *Bouncing back: Rebuilding resilient supply chains.* Organisation for Economic Co-operation and Development.
6. Gowan, R., & Yazigi, J. (2020). *Economic interdependence and national security in an age of rivalry.* European Council on Foreign Relations.
7. Rodrik, D. (2018). What do trade agreements really do? *Journal of Economic Perspectives, 32*(2), 73–90.

CHAPTER 2

DEFINING RESILIENCE IN THE ECONOMIC SPHERE

The word *resilience* is now everywhere. Governments promise it, institutions publish strategies about it, and companies add it to their presentations. But the more widely the term is used, the less clear it can become. If everything is resilience, nothing is. For Resilient Trade Theory (RTT) to be useful, resilience needs a sharper definition, one that distinguishes it from self-sufficiency, from simple redundancy, and from vague calls to "be prepared."

This chapter sets out what resilience means in the economic sphere, and what it does not. It treats resilience as a multidimensional property of systems—economic, social, and geopolitical, that shows up not in slogans, but in how a country behaves under pressure. It also clarifies how **strategic autonomy** differs from **absolute self-sufficiency**, and why that distinction matters for both policy and scholarship.

The goal is straightforward: by the end of this chapter, resilience should no longer be a loose aspiration. It should be a working concept that can guide decisions in trade, industrial policy, labour, and diplomacy.

1. Resilience as a Multidimensional Property

Resilience is often defined, in simple terms, as the ability to "bounce back" after a shock. In complex systems, that description is incomplete. Some shocks are absorbed. Some are deflected. Some are adapted to, permanently. And in some cases, the goal is not to bounce back to where we were, but to transition to a more stable configuration.[1]

For the purposes of RTT, three dimensions matter: **economic resilience**, **social resilience**, and **geopolitical resilience**. They are distinct, but they interact.

Economic Resilience

Economic resilience is the capacity of an economy to sustain and restore essential functions when confronted with shocks. That includes the ability to:

- Maintain basic flows, food, energy, healthcare, water, digital connectivity, and core logistics.
- Reallocate resources quickly when specific nodes fail (for example, rerouting trade through alternative ports or suppliers).
- Substitute inputs or processes when original sources are disrupted.
- Recover production capacity within a timeframe that society can tolerate.

An economy that cannot ensure these basic functions is not simply inefficient. It becomes vulnerable to cascading failures and social instability.

Social Resilience

Social resilience refers to the ability of communities and institutions to absorb stress without fragmenting. It is reflected in:

- Public trust in institutions, especially during crisis.
- The willingness of workers to continue operating essential systems under strain.
- The absence of large-scale unrest when temporary constraints (for example, rationing) are necessary.
- The density of local networks, SMEs, cooperatives, community organisations, that can improvise and support continuity when central systems struggle.[2]

Without social resilience, even well-designed technical systems can fail. People must be willing to follow emergency rules, accept temporary burdens, and sustain cooperation. That is more likely when they believe the system is broadly fair and when those asking for sacrifice have invested in their security in advance.

Geopolitical Resilience

Geopolitical resilience is the ability of a state or bloc to withstand external pressure without being forced into choices that undermine its core interests or values. In practice, this depends heavily on the structure of trade, finance, and technology relationships. It involves:

- Limiting exposure to critical inputs that can be easily weaponised.
- Building allied networks that can provide support in times of stress.

- Retaining enough internal capacity in essentials to avoid immediate capitulation when threatened.
- Ensuring that dependence on others is reciprocal and structured, rather than one-sided and exploitable.[3]

Resilience in this dimension does not mean avoiding all dependence. It means designing dependence so that it cannot be used as a simple lever of coercion.

These three dimensions overlap. A country that cannot keep its hospital system supplied is economically fragile, but it is also socially and geopolitically vulnerable. A country that ignores labour conditions in essential sectors may find that its "resilient" infrastructure is unsupported when it is needed most. An accurate understanding of resilience must keep these linkages in view.

2. Resilience vs. Autarky

One of the most common misunderstandings is to equate resilience with autarky. The two are not the same.

Autarky aims at comprehensive self-sufficiency. It minimises reliance on external trade across a wide range of sectors, often for ideological or security reasons. In its extreme forms, it accepts significant economic costs, higher prices, slower innovation, lower variety, in exchange for reduced exposure to external influence.

RTT does not advocate autarky. It starts from a different premise: that **interdependence is a structural reality**, but that it should be shaped, not simply accepted as given. Resilience seeks to:

- Ensure that in *essential sectors* a country can maintain continuity under stress through a mix of domestic capacity, allied support, and reserves.

- Accept and even encourage deep openness in *non-essential sectors* where the consequences of disruption are far less severe.
- Use trade and cooperation to improve resilience, not just to maximise throughput.

In other words, resilience is **selective**. It directs attention and investment to parts of the system where failure would be existential or severely destabilising. It does not attempt to reproduce that level of protection everywhere.

There are clear reasons to avoid autarky as a general strategy:

- It can be prohibitively expensive, especially for smaller economies.
- It can limit access to knowledge, technology, and capital.
- It can foster insularity and weaken alliances.
- It can be used to justify political control and lack of accountability.

Resilience, in contrast, is compatible with openness and cooperation. It places boundaries around where self-sufficiency is necessary and where it is not. It accepts that some forms of dependence are not only tolerable, but desirable, provided they are not concentrated in sectors where failure would be catastrophic.

3. Resilience vs. Redundancy

Resilience is also more than simple redundancy. Redundancy, having more than one of something, can be a component of resilience, but it is not sufficient on its own.

A system can have multiple suppliers, multiple routes, or multiple facilities and still be fragile if:

- All redundant options are exposed to the same hazard (for example, several ports on the same vulnerable coastline).
- The redundancy is poorly integrated (additional capacity exists but cannot be activated quickly).
- Social or political factors block the use of backup options when they are needed.
- Critical skills are concentrated in too few people or organisations.

RTT is interested in what might be called **purposeful redundancy**: additional capacity, pathways, or options that are specifically designed to:

- Operate under conditions of stress (heat, conflict, cyber disruption).
- Be mobilised within the time window that matters.
- Be geographically, politically, or technologically distinct enough that they are unlikely to fail for the same reason.
- Be sustained over time without imposing unnecessary costs on the rest of the economy.[4]

The objective is not to duplicate everything. It is to ensure that for each essential function, at least one credible alternative exists that can be activated when primary systems fail. That can mean maintaining reserve capacity in domestic production, securing pre-agreed access to allied capacity, or holding stockpiles that bridge the gap between disruption and recovery.

Resilience also includes the ability to **adapt**, to change processes, re-route flows, or substitute inputs when conditions require it. Redundancy without adaptability can simply delay failure. Resilience seeks to avoid failure, manage it when it occurs, and emerge from it with informed adjustments.

4. Strategic Autonomy vs. Absolute Self-Sufficiency

The European Union has popularised the language of "strategic autonomy" to describe its attempt to reduce vulnerabilities in critical areas while remaining open to trade and cooperation.[5] This language is useful, but it is often interpreted in different ways.

Absolute self-sufficiency suggests that a country should be able to provide for its needs internally, with minimal reliance on external partners. This is close to the autarkic concept discussed earlier.

Strategic autonomy, as used in RTT, means something more modest and more achievable: the ability to make key decisions, economic, security-related, and political, without being forced into them by the threat of supply disruption or coercive leverage over critical systems.

This form of autonomy can be secured in different ways:

- By retaining a domestic "anchor" capacity in critical sectors, even if much of the production is internationalised.
- By diversifying suppliers and routes so that no single actor can exercise decisive pressure.
- By embedding continuity obligations and emergency cooperation mechanisms into trade agreements.
- By coordinating with allies to create resilience blocs and shared reserves.

Strategic autonomy is therefore **relational**, not solitary. It accepts that in an integrated world some dependencies will always exist. It focuses on shaping those dependencies so that they do not translate easily into coercion.

Absolute self-sufficiency, by contrast, is rarely realistic beyond a narrow set of sectors or in the most extreme security environments. Attempting to extend it broadly would impose costs that few societies would accept in peacetime.

5. Case Windows: When Resilience Failed and When It Helped

Definitions become more tangible when attached to experience. Two brief cases can illustrate what resilience is, and is not, in practice.

Failure Case: Medical Supply During COVID-19

When COVID-19 struck, many countries discovered that basic medical supplies, masks, gloves, gowns, and in some cases even oxygen and ventilator components, were heavily dependent on a small number of manufacturing hubs and export routes.[6] As demand spiked, some producer states limited exports. Logistics systems slowed or seized. National governments competed for the same small pool of goods.

In resilience terms, several weaknesses became visible:

- Essential goods had not been clearly distinguished, in policy, from non-essential goods.
- Stockpiles were inadequate or had not been maintained.
- Supplier bases were geographically concentrated.
- Emergency procurement and substitution procedures were improvised, not pre-planned.

This was not a failure of trade per se. Global production had, in ordinary times, supplied large volumes at low cost. It was a failure to recognise that for certain goods, normal-time efficiency needed to be balanced with crisis-time continuity. RTT responds by treating specific medical items as part of an essential sector with its own rules, reserves, diversified suppliers, allied production agreements, and clear triggers for scaling up.

Partial Success: Civil Preparedness in a Nordic Context

By contrast, some countries with long-standing civil defence traditions had maintained broad-based preparedness measures: distributed food and fuel reserves, decentralised energy systems, and regular exercises involving both public authorities and private operators.[7]

When disruptions occurred, whether from storms, cyber incidents, or supply interruptions, these countries could draw on:

- Pre-positioned stocks in multiple locations.
- Local decision-making capacity at municipal or regional levels.
- Populations familiar with basic preparedness expectations.
- Established channels for coordinating between central government, businesses, and civil society.

These arrangements did not prevent shocks, and they did not remove all economic damage. But they often prevented shocks from becoming crises. They show resilience as a lived practice, not simply as a stated goal.

These examples are not presented as ideal models. They simply illustrate how differences in classification, preparation, and institutional practice can produce very different outcomes when stress arrives.

6. Exhibit: A Working Typology of Resilience

To make the concept more operational, it is helpful to summarise the distinctions discussed above.

Exhibit 2 - Typology of Resilience Terms

Term	Core idea	Risk of confusion
Resilience	Ability to maintain and restore essential functions under stress, and to adapt	Often used so broadly that it loses operational meaning
Autarky	Minimisation of trade and external dependence across many sectors	Can be mistaken for resilience, but is much broader and more costly
Redundancy	Having more than one of a given asset, route, or supplier	Useful, but not sufficient if all options share the same vulnerabilities
Strategic autonomy	Capacity to make key decisions without being forced by external leverage over essentials	Can be misread as a call for general self-sufficiency

RTT uses resilience in the narrower, operational sense: focused on **essential sectors**, attentive to **time frames**, and interested in **practical design choices** rather than abstract robustness.

7. A Practical Test: Are We Talking About Resilience or Something Else?

To prevent drift in policy discussions, it is useful to have a simple test.

Toolkit 2 - Seven Questions to Test "Resilience" Measures

1. Does the measure clearly specify which essential sector or function it is protecting?
2. Does it identify the main shocks or pressures it is meant to respond to?
3. Does it operate within a defined timeframe, how long it can bridge a disruption, or how quickly it can be activated?
4. Does it rely on purposeful redundancy (distinct options) rather than simple duplication of the same vulnerability?
5. Does it include a role for allied cooperation where appropriate, or does it default to self-sufficiency without justification?
6. Does it interact with social factors, labour conditions, trust, communication, in a way that supports continuity?
7. Does it have a review or sunset mechanism, so that it can be adjusted or withdrawn if circumstances change?

A measure that cannot answer these questions is not necessarily wrong. But it should not be described as a resilience policy. It may be industrial policy, distributional policy, or foreign policy under another name. Clarity about terms helps keep debates honest and expectations realistic.

8. Conclusion: From Concept to Design

This chapter has argued that resilience, in the context of trade and economic policy, is not a synonym for self-sufficiency, nor for redundancy, nor for vague robustness. It is a specific property: the ability to maintain and restore essential functions under stress, and to adapt structures in light of experience.

Resilience differs from autarky in that it is selective and open to cooperation. It differs from simple redundancy in that it cares about distinct vulnerabilities, timeframes, and institutional capacity. Strategic autonomy, in this framework, is not about standing alone; it is about ensuring that no single external actor can decisively compromise a country's essential systems.

In the chapters that follow, these concepts will be applied more concretely. We will examine the ethical foundations of Resilient Trade Theory, the obligations states have to protect their populations and future generations. We will then move to the structure of RTT: how to classify sectors, design capacity, govern trade, and build alliances that support continuity rather than undermine it.

Resilience is not simply a descriptive term. It is a choice about how to structure interdependence. To make that choice thoughtfully, the concept must be precise. That is the purpose of defining it carefully here, before moving on to the more difficult work of designing and implementing it.

Endnotes

1. Holling, C. S. (1973). Resilience and stability of ecological systems. *Annual Review of Ecology and Systematics, 4*, 1–23.
2. Adger, W. N. (2000). Social and ecological resilience: Are they related? *Progress in Human Geography, 24*(3), 347–364.
3. Farrell, H., & Newman, A. L. (2019). Weaponized interdependence: How global economic networks shape state coercion. *International Security, 44*(1), 42–79.

4. WTO. (2021). *World Trade Report 2021: Economic resilience and trade.* World Trade Organization.
5. European Commission. (2021–2023). Communications on *Open Strategic Autonomy* and updated industrial strategy.
6. OECD. (2021). *Bouncing back: Rebuilding resilient supply chains.* Organisation for Economic Co-operation and Development.
7. National Academies of Sciences, Engineering, and Medicine. (2022). *Building Resilient Supply Chains: A Strategy for Strengthening U.S. Resilience.*

CHAPTER 3

ETHICS, SOVEREIGNTY, AND THE MORAL IMPERATIVE

Economic debates are often framed as technical questions: growth rates, price levels, trade balances, productivity. Ethical considerations sit in the background, acknowledged but rarely placed at the centre of analysis. Resilient Trade Theory (RTT) takes a different approach. It begins from a simple claim: **how a state structures its trade and production systems is not only an economic choice, but a moral one**.

When basic goods fail, food, energy, medicine, clean water, secure communications, the consequences are not abstract. They fall on specific people in specific places, and they fall unevenly. When a state allows essential sectors to remain fragile, it is not simply accepting risk. It is implicitly deciding who will bear the cost when systems break.

This chapter develops the ethical foundations of RTT. It treats trade as a moral instrument, not just a vehicle for efficiency. It argues that states have a duty not only to pursue growth, but to provide **continuity**, the ability of their societies to function under stress. It explores questions of justice across class, region, and generation. And it makes the case that securing essential capacities is not a luxury for wealthy states, but part of the basic responsibilities of governance.

1. Trade as a Moral Instrument, Not Just an Economic Tool

Modern trade theory is often presented as value-neutral: given preferences and technologies, we ask how to maximise welfare under certain constraints. But in practice, trade policy involves choices about exposure, dependence, and distribution that are inherently normative. The location of production, the depth of integration, and the design of agreements all create patterns of vulnerability as well as patterns of gain.

Two points are central.

First, **the benefits and risks of trade are distributed unevenly**. Export-led growth in one region may coincide with deindustrialisation in another. Offshoring may lower aggregate prices while undermining local employment and eroding skills. Concentrating pharmaceutical or semiconductor production in a handful of sites may reduce costs, but it also concentrates risk.[1] The choice to prioritise efficiency without regard to resilience is therefore a choice about whose security is being discounted.

Second, **trade architecture shapes power**. States with control over critical nodes, ports, payment systems, standards, or rare inputs, can exert leverage over others. This leverage can be used responsibly or irresponsibly, but it exists either way. The question for policy is whether that leverage is taken for granted, or whether we attempt to design systems that reduce the scope for coercion.

RTT treats trade as a moral instrument in three ways:

- It asks **which dependencies are acceptable**, and which place unacceptable power in the hands of external actors.
- It asks **whose livelihoods and regions are being rendered expendable** by efficiency-only logic.

- It asks **how the gains from trade can be balanced with the duty to provide continuity** when conditions turn adverse.

Economic models can help illuminate trade-offs, but they cannot, on their own, decide which risks or harms are tolerable. Those are ethical questions.

2. The Duty of States: Continuity, Not Just Growth

States are judged by many metrics: GDP growth, employment, inflation, fiscal balance, governance indicators. RTT adds another: **the ability to protect basic life-supporting systems under stress.**

At minimum, citizens can reasonably expect their governments to:

- Safeguard access to food, water, and energy.
- Keep health systems functioning in crisis.
- Maintain essential communications and public order.
- Protect the institutional core of democratic decision-making.

Growth can help make this easier. But high GDP is not, on its own, a guarantee of continuity. In some cases, it can mask fragility by encouraging overconfidence and underinvestment in basic resilience.[2]

From an ethical perspective, the duty of the state is twofold:

1. **Prevent avoidable breakdowns.** If foreseeable risks are ignored and critical sectors are left exposed when there were feasible options to mitigate them, the resulting harms are not accidents. They are failures of care.
2. **Manage unavoidable shocks fairly.** Some disruptions cannot be prevented. But states can decide in advance how

they will allocate scarce goods, who will be prioritised, and how burdens will be shared. Transparent, pre-agreed rules are more legitimate than improvised reactions shaped by political pressure.

RTT operationalises this duty through instruments such as essential sector registers, strategic sufficiency thresholds, stockpiles, protected corridors, and continuity clauses. These are not merely technical devices. They are expressions of responsibility.

Exhibit 1 - Two Responsibilities of a Resilient State

- **Responsibility ex ante:** Design systems so that foreseeable shocks are unlikely to cause collapse in essentials.
- **Responsibility ex post:** When shocks occur, allocate scarcity and adjust systems in ways that are as fair, transparent, and predictable as possible.

The ethical claim is modest, but demanding. States do not have to anticipate every contingency, but they do have to treat essential systems as matters of duty, not as residuals of wider economic logic.

3. Justice Across Class and Region

Resilience failures have a distributional pattern. They rarely fall evenly across a society.

When energy prices spike, it is low-income households and small firms that struggle most. When supply chains fail, it is often those on insecure contracts, in peripheral regions, or in small and medium-sized enterprises that bear the brunt. When food or medicine runs short, it is marginalised communities that are least able to buffer the shock.

Three mechanisms matter here.

Unequal Vulnerability

Some groups depend more directly on public systems than others. Wealthy households can install generators, maintain private water supplies, or purchase services abroad. Large firms can diversify globally. By contrast, those without savings or mobility are directly exposed to the robustness of national systems.[3]

This creates a basic justice concern: **if essential sectors are left fragile, the costs of that fragility will fall disproportionately on those least able to bear them.** RTT responds by arguing that resilience investments in essentials, stockpiles, local nodes, robust public infrastructure, are implicitly progressive, because they secure goods that cannot be easily substituted privately.

Unequal Voice

Communities that lose from efficiency-first policy often have limited influence over trade and industrial decisions. Rural regions affected by agricultural import competition, industrial towns hollowed out by offshoring, and small island or border communities exposed to supply interruptions typically do not sit at negotiating tables.

RTT does not claim to solve this problem entirely. But it does argue for **inclusive planning** in essential sectors, structured consultation processes, community involvement in siting decisions, and transparency mechanisms that allow those most affected to understand and contest decisions.

Unequal Employment Options

When domestic production in essential sectors is hollowed out, the quality of remaining jobs can deteriorate. Supply chains may become more precarious. Wages can stagnate. In some regions, especially those excluded from service-sector growth, the erosion of foundational industries is experienced as abandonment.

The ethical response, within RTT, is to treat **labour in essential sectors as part of national security**. A minimum liveable wage, decent working conditions, and investment in skills are not purely social policy, they are conditions for having people who are willing and able to keep systems running when stress arrives.

4. Justice Across Generations

There is also a temporal dimension. Choices made now about trade and production structure will shape the options available to future generations.

If a country allows its capacity in essential sectors to erode, to the point where skills are lost, supply chains are hollow, and critical infrastructure is dependent on single external sources, it is not only putting current citizens at risk. It is handing future citizens a brittle system that will be more expensive and more difficult to repair.

By contrast, investments in resilience, if well designed, have a long life. Grain reserves, diversified corridors, domestic anchor facilities, robust local grids, and knowledge institutions in agriculture, health, and engineering all provide **option value**. They give future decision-makers more room to manoeuvre.[4]

Treating resilience as a moral commitment across generations yields three practical implications:

- **Do not consume resilience capital as if it were income.** Running down stockpiles, underfunding maintenance, or closing training pipelines to save money today simply shifts cost and risk to tomorrow.
- **Build capacities that are adaptable.** Infrastructure and institutions should be designed so that they can evolve as technologies and risks change.
- **Involve younger voices in planning.** If resilience policy is made entirely by those who will not live with its long-term consequences, it risks underweighting future harms.

The intergenerational argument is not abstract. Climate change itself is a case of long-lived externality. A fragile trade architecture layered on top of climate stress is an additional burden that future citizens will have to carry. RTT is one way of reducing that burden, by ensuring that essential systems are not left in a condition of unmanaged vulnerability.

5. Sovereignty as Responsibility, Not Isolation

Sovereignty is sometimes cast as freedom from external constraint. In practice, it is more useful to think of sovereignty as **responsibility for a defined community and territory**. That responsibility includes the duty to avoid exposing the population to unnecessary risk from external decisions.

When a state becomes heavily dependent for food, energy, or critical technologies on actors that do not share its interests or values, it implicitly transfers part of its sovereignty to those actors. They may never exercise that leverage. But the latent possibility alters the calculations of both sides.[5]

RTT frames sovereignty in the following way:

- A sovereign state has the right to participate in trade and cooperation on terms that do not require it to abandon its capacity to protect its population.
- A sovereign state has the obligation to prevent foreseeable external leverage over essential systems where viable alternatives exist.
- A sovereign state should, where possible, structure its interdependence in allied and rule-bound ways, so that mutual obligations are clear and enforceable.

This view is not hostile to globalisation. It simply insists that **openness must not come at the price of losing control over the basic conditions of social survival**. Trade remains a central instrument of prosperity. It cannot be the sole pillar of security.

6. Exhibit: Ethical Questions for Essential Sector Policy

To translate these considerations into practice, policymakers need concrete questions. The following can serve as a starting checklist.

Exhibit 2 - Ethical Questions for Essential Sectors

1. **Exposure:** Are we placing control over essential goods or services in the hands of actors whose interests may diverge sharply from ours?
2. **Distribution:** If a failure occurs, which groups and regions will be most affected, and have we consulted them in advance?
3. **Alternatives:** Have we explored reasonable options for diversification, allied cooperation, or localised capacity before accepting high-risk dependencies?

4. **Transparency:** Do citizens understand the trade-offs we have made, and can they access information about vulnerabilities and plans?
5. **Labour:** Are the people who run essential systems treated in a way that reflects their importance, or are they among the most precarious in the economy?
6. **Future impact:** Will this decision leave future governments with more options, or fewer? Are we drawing down resilience that will be hard to rebuild?

These questions do not yield automatic answers. They do, however, help prevent ethical issues from being treated as afterthoughts in what might otherwise be a purely technocratic discussion.

7. The Ethical Case for Securing Essential Capacities

Bringing these strands together, we can state the ethical case for RTT in straightforward terms.

1. **Protection of life and basic welfare.** States have a primary duty to protect their populations from avoidable harm. Ensuring continuity in essential sectors is part of that duty. Leaving those sectors fragile, when there are feasible ways to strengthen them, is a failure of care.[6]
2. **Fair distribution of risk.** An efficiency-only strategy that generates fragility imposes disproportionate risk on those with least wealth and least mobility. Resilience investments in essentials help level this asymmetry by providing public goods that cannot be replicated privately.
3. **Preservation of democratic agency.** When states lack strategic autonomy in essentials, they may be compelled to accept choices under threat, choices that their citizens

would not freely endorse. Securing essential capacities protects not only material welfare, but the integrity of democratic decision-making.

4. **Intergenerational stewardship.** Future citizens cannot vote in present debates. Treating resilience as a long-lived asset respects their interests by avoiding the handover of brittle systems that are expensive or impossible to repair.
5. **Responsible participation in interdependence.** By designing trade in ways that promote continuity and reduce temptation for coercion, states contribute to a more stable international environment. Resilience blocs, continuity clauses, and shared reserves can make cooperation more durable, not less.

These ethical foundations do not specify the exact mix of policies a given country should adopt. They provide a compass: secure essentials; avoid unjust burdens; preserve choice; think beyond one electoral cycle.

8. Toolkit: Normative Guidelines for Resilient Trade Theory

To make the moral logic of RTT usable in everyday policy work, it is helpful to translate it into a short set of guidelines.

Toolkit 3 - Normative Guidelines for Resilient Trade

- **Name the essentials.** Do not leave "vital sectors" implicit. Identify them publicly and explain why they are treated differently.
- **Justify dependencies.** If an essential sector relies heavily on external sources, explain why. Show that alternatives have been considered and that the remaining risk is acceptable.

- **Protect the backbone.** Ensure that workers in essential sectors receive liveable wages, training, and basic security. If they cannot afford to stay, the system will not hold.
- **Design for allies, not just markets.** Use trade agreements to embed continuity obligations, crisis procedures, and joint preparedness in essentials. Partner choice is an ethical decision.
- **Share information.** Publish resilience audits and scenario plans in accessible form. Trust depends on visible preparation, not just assurances.
- **Plan for those most at risk.** When designing rationing rules or emergency measures, start from the perspective of those with least margin low-income households, remote regions, and institutions that serve them.
- **Protect the future.** Treat stockpiles, skills, and infrastructure in essentials as long-lived assets. Avoid policies that offer short-term savings at the cost of long-term fragility.

These guidelines are not a substitute for economic analysis. They are a set of ethical constraints and priorities to sit alongside it.

9. Conclusion: From Obligation to Design

Resilient Trade Theory is not morally neutral. It rests on the claim that states have an obligation to ensure continuity in essential sectors, to distribute risk fairly, and to preserve their capacity for independent decision-making in the face of external pressure. It asserts that trade policy, industrial strategy, and labour policy cannot be evaluated solely by their contribution to growth or efficiency. They must also be judged by their contribution to, or erosion of, resilience.

This chapter has argued that resilience is not simply a technical improvement. It is an ethical stance that recognises the uneven impact of fragility across class, region, and generation. It reframes sovereignty as responsibility for safeguarding essential systems, not as a desire to withdraw from the world. It urges policymakers and scholars to see trade architecture as part of the moral infrastructure of the state.

In the chapters that follow, this ethical frame will be linked to the structural components of RTT: how to classify sectors, design capacity, build institutions, and negotiate alliances. If the ethical case is accepted, the question is no longer whether resilience should be pursued, but how to do so in ways that are effective, transparent, and compatible with an open, innovative global economy.

Endnotes

1. WTO. (2021). *World Trade Report 2021: Economic resilience and trade.* World Trade Organization.
2. IMF. (2023). *Geoeconomic fragmentation and the future of multilateralism.* International Monetary Fund.
3. OECD. (2021). *Bouncing back: Rebuilding resilient supply chains.* Organisation for Economic Co-operation and Development.
4. National Academies of Sciences, Engineering, and Medicine. (2022). *Building Resilient Supply Chains: A Strategy for Strengthening U.S. Resilience.*
5. Farrell, H., & Newman, A. L. (2019). Weaponized interdependence: How global economic networks shape state coercion. *International Security, 44*(1), 42–79.
6. Pogge, T. (2002). *World Poverty and Human Rights.* Polity Press.

PART II

The Structure of Resilient Trade Theory

CHAPTER 4

THE STRATEGIC CATEGORISATION OF GOODS AND SECTORS

Resilient Trade Theory (RTT) stands or falls on one basic task: deciding which parts of the economy are truly essential, and which are not. Unless that line is drawn with care, everything risks being labelled “strategic,” and the framework collapses into unfocused protectionism. If, on the other hand, the line is drawn too narrowly or left vague, essential sectors remain exposed in practice while being protected only in rhetoric.

This chapter addresses that foundational step. It sets out a structured way to **categorise goods and sectors**, distinguishes **essential from non-essential**, explains why a **tiered approach** is preferable to a simple binary, and describes how to build a **living Essentiality Register** that can change as technologies and geopolitics change. It then turns to **vulnerability mapping** and **interdependence stress-testing**, tools that transform classification from a label into an operational guide for policy.

The objective is practical: to move from intuition (“this feels strategic”) to a repeatable process that can be scrutinised, contested, and improved.

1. Why Classification Is a Precondition for Resilience

Resilience is often invoked as a general aspiration. But without clear classification, it cannot be implemented. A state that does not know which sectors are essential cannot meaningfully:

- Prioritise investment and capacity-building.
- Design differentiated trade rules.
- Decide where redundancy is warranted and where it is wasteful.
- Communicate to citizens why some sectors receive special treatment.

By contrast, a state that has a well-defined classification can:

- Focus scarce fiscal and administrative resources on high-impact vulnerabilities.
- Explain why certain measures, stockpiles, subsidies, allied sourcing, apply to some sectors and not others.
- Use a common language across ministries, agencies, and partners.
- Evaluate whether resilience is improving or deteriorating in specific areas.[1]

Classification is therefore not a marginal technical exercise. It is the **starting point of resilient trade**. It shapes the rest of the framework: capacity, labour strategy, governance, and diplomacy.

2. Essential vs. Non-Essential: Criteria, Not Intuition

In everyday language, "essential" is often used informally. In policy design, that is not enough. RTT proposes that sectors be assessed against a set of **criteria**, rather than on the basis of political influence or habit.

Core Criteria

At minimum, classification should consider:

1. **Impact on life and basic welfare**
    - Does disruption directly threaten health, food security, access to water, shelter, or basic safety?
2. **Systemic centrality**
    - Does the sector support multiple other sectors (for example, energy, digital infrastructure, logistics, finance)? Does its failure propagate widely?
3. **Substitutability**
    - Can goods or services from this sector be substituted easily, either by imports from alternative sources or by different technologies? How long would substitution take?
4. **Time sensitivity**
    - How quickly would disruption become critical? Hours, days, weeks, months? What are the "time-to-survive" and "time-to-recover" intervals?
5. **Geopolitical leverage potential**
    - Could control over this sector or its key inputs be used coercively by external actors?
6. **Reversibility of loss**
    - If capacity is lost (skills, facilities, tooling), how difficult and time-consuming would it be to rebuild?[2]

A sector that scores high on several of these criteria is a candidate for "essential" status. A sector that scores low on all of them is likely to be "non-essential" for the purposes of RTT, even if it is economically important.

From Binary to Tiers

A simple essential/non-essential binary can still be too coarse to guide policy. RTT therefore suggests a **tiered** classification:

- **Tier 1: Lifeline sectors.**

  Immediate survival and public order depend on these: staple food systems, core energy and grid equipment, drinking water and sanitation, critical healthcare goods and services, secure digital backbones, and certain defence inputs.

- **Tier 2: Enabling sectors.**

  These sectors are not directly life-supporting but are required to keep Tier 1 functioning: key logistics nodes, specialised chemicals, industrial gases, certain metals and components, repair and maintenance ecosystems, testing and metrology services.

- **Tier 3: Important but non-essential sectors.**

  These contribute strongly to output and employment but do not cause immediate systemic breakdown if disrupted: most consumer goods, non-core services, many manufacturing activities.

- **Tier 4: Discretionary and luxury sectors.**

  High-value but low-criticality sectors: luxury goods, entertainment products, non-essential tourism niches, and similar activities.

This tiering does not deny the economic value of Tier 3 and 4. It simply recognises that, in designing resilience, Tier 1 and Tier 2 must receive different treatment.

Exhibit 1 - Illustrative Tier Mapping (Simplified)

- **Tier 1:** Wheat and rice seed systems; electricity transmission equipment; water treatment membranes; antibiotics, insulin, vaccines; core telecom networks; air traffic control; defence logistics.
- **Tier 2:** Fertilizers, key feed grains; transformer components; industrial gases for chip production; pharmaceutical precursors; major ports and rail hubs; cloud and data centre infrastructure.
- **Tier 3:** Consumer electronics assembly; automotive exports; furniture; non-essential apparel.
- **Tier 4:** Luxury fashion; high-end tourism; entertainment streaming; fine wines and spirits.

Each country or bloc will populate these tiers differently. The point is not to fix one universal list, but to **use structured criteria** rather than ad hoc designation.

3. Building an Essentiality Register

Once classification criteria and tiers are agreed, they should be codified in an **Essentiality Register**, a structured inventory of sectors and critical goods, with clear justifications.

Elements of a Robust Register

A credible register should include, at minimum:

- **Sector name and scope** (e.g., "APIs for selected anti-infectives" rather than "pharma" in general).
- **Tier designation** (1–4) and key criteria that support the designation.

- **Key functions** the sector supports (e.g., "ICU capacity," "grid stability," "drinking water safety").
- **Primary supply routes and sources**, domestic and foreign.
- **Known chokepoints** (single points of failure, concentration of suppliers, critical inputs).
- **Indicative strategic sufficiency target**, such as minimum days of stock, minimum domestic or allied capacity share, or maximum acceptable supplier concentration.[3]

The register should be developed through a **cross-ministerial process**, led by the Resilient Trade Authority (or equivalent) and involving line ministries (agriculture, energy, health, defence, digital, transport), central banks where relevant, and regulatory agencies. It should also draw on external expertise from industry, academia, and civil society.

Governance of the Register

The Essentiality Register should:

- Be approved at cabinet level or by the relevant political authority.
- Be updated regularly (for example, annually) with a documented review process.
- Be published in an accessible form, with sensitive details protected but core classifications visible.
- Include a mechanism for stakeholders to propose reclassification or additions based on evidence.

Publication is important for legitimacy. Citizens and firms are more likely to accept differentiated treatment across sectors if they can see the logic. Transparency also helps limit lobbying for "strategic" status on weak grounds.

4. Dynamic Classification: Adapting to Change

Classification cannot be static. Technologies evolve, new dependencies emerge, climate impacts shift hazard maps, and geopolitical alignments change. A sector that is non-essential today may become essential tomorrow; a sector that is currently strategic may become less so if substitutes become widely available.

RTT therefore treats classification as **dynamic**, guided by both periodic review and specific triggers.

Periodic Review

Regular reviews, every 12–24 months, serve to:

- Reassess sectors against the core criteria in light of new data.
- Incorporate technological innovations (e.g., new energy storage, new medical platforms).
- Reflect changes in trade patterns (e.g., new suppliers, new corridors).
- Adjust strategic sufficiency targets based on experience.

These reviews should be documented, with explanations for major changes, so that classification does not drift without rationale.

Trigger-Based Updates

In addition to scheduled reviews, certain events should automatically prompt re-examination of relevant sectors:

- **Major shocks** (pandemic, war, climate event, cyberattack) that expose previously underappreciated vulnerabilities.
- **Technological breakthroughs** that reduce dependence on scarce inputs or single suppliers.

- **Geopolitical shifts** (alliances, sanctions, export control regimes) that change the availability of critical goods.
- **Market concentration changes** (e.g., mergers or closures) that increase or decrease systemic risk.[4]

Trigger-based updates ensure that the classification system reacts to reality, rather than being a static list that slowly diverges from actual risk.

Exhibit 2 - Example of Dynamic Reclassification

- Before a pandemic, generic mask production may be classified as Tier 3, important but non-essential.
- After a pandemic reveals widespread shortages and dependence on a small number of offshore suppliers, a government may reclassify specific PPE items as Tier 1 or Tier 2, with associated targets for domestic capacity, stockpiles, and allied sourcing.

The lesson is not to declare everything essential after a crisis, but to integrate experience into a disciplined and transparent reclassification process.

5. Vulnerability Mapping: From Lists to Networks

Classification tells us **what** matters. Vulnerability mapping begins to show **how** it can fail.

A vulnerability map is not just a list of risks. It is a representation of relationships: which sectors depend on which inputs, which routes connect which nodes, and where concentration creates leverage.

Key Elements of Vulnerability Mapping

A useful mapping exercise includes:

- **Supply chain mapping** for Tier 1 and 2 sectors: upstream inputs, processing nodes, logistics steps, and downstream dependencies.
- **Geographic overlay**: where key nodes are located (domestically and abroad), and what hazards they face (flood, drought, conflict, seismic risk, political instability).
- **Ownership and control**: who owns or controls critical nodes (state, foreign firms, consortia), and what legal or political leverage exists.
- **Substitution pathways**: what alternatives exist if a node fails, alternate suppliers, alternate routes, alternate technologies, and how long they would take to activate.[5]

The output does not need to be a perfect model. Even a simplified map can reveal concentration that was not obvious, or dependencies on jurisdictions with high political or climate risk.

Chokepoints and Single Points of Failure

Within the map, the Resilient Trade Authority should identify **chokepoints**, assets or routes whose failure would cause disproportionate harm and for which substitutes are limited or slow.

Examples include:

- A handful of factories producing key active pharmaceutical ingredients.
- A limited number of facilities that manufacture high-voltage transformers.

- A small set of export terminals handling the bulk of grain or fertilizer shipments.
- A single undersea cable or satellite link serving an island state.

For each chokepoint, two questions should be asked:

1. **How likely is disruption?** (Given hazards, political context, cyber exposure.)
2. **How quickly can we recover or reroute?** (Given alternative capacity, stockpiles, and agreements.)

These questions directly inform where capacity-building and trade diversification efforts should focus.

6. Interdependence Stress-Testing

Stress-testing takes vulnerability mapping one step further. Rather than simply describing the system, it asks: **What happens under specific scenarios?**

Stress-tests simulate shocks, climate events, cyber incidents, export bans, port closures, and trace their impact through the network of essential sectors.[6] They can be conducted through table-top exercises, models, or hybrids of both.

Types of Stress-Tests

RTT encourages three families of tests:

1. **Single-shock tests**
   - Example: closure of a major port due to a storm; an export ban on a critical input; a cyberattack on a major distributor.
   - Purpose: understand immediate impacts and test contingency plans.

2. **Compound-shock tests**
   - Example: drought reducing river traffic combined with a cyberattack on a rail operator; a pandemic coinciding with a heat wave that strains energy systems.
   - Purpose: reflect the reality that shocks often interact rather than occur in isolation.
3. **Geopolitical stress-tests**
   - Example: a major supplier country imposing export controls; a regional conflict disrupting airspace and shipping lanes.
   - Purpose: evaluate resilience of allied corridors and the credibility of continuity clauses.

Each stress-test should generate specific findings: which sectors are most exposed, which chokepoints create disproportionate impacts, where stockpiles are inadequate, and which bilateral or multilateral arrangements prove brittle.

Regional Illustrations

- **East Asia (technology and energy)**: Stress-tests might examine the impact of a disruption in semiconductor production in Taiwan or of fuel supply constraints in a regional conflict, and how quickly alternative capacity in Japan, Korea, or the United States could compensate.
- **Europe (agriculture and energy)**: Tests might explore river-level drops affecting grain exports, combined with gas supply interruptions, and measure how quickly intra-EU corridors and reserves can respond.
- **Latin America (agriculture and fertilizers)**: Scenarios might consider port closures due to storms, combined with import delays for fertilizers, and assess effects on planting seasons and food security in importing regions.

The goal is not to generate fear, but to **pressure-test the classification and capacity-building choices** made under RTT. A sector that is classified as Tier 1 but fails consistently in stress-tests needs more attention. A sector that remains robust under multiple scenarios might be a candidate for relaxed measures.

7. Exhibit: A Simple Classification and Stress-Testing Process

To make this concrete, it helps to visualise the process as a sequence.

Exhibit 3 - From Classification to Stress-Testing

1. **Define criteria** for essentiality and agree on a tier structure.
2. **Populate the Essentiality Register** with sectors and key goods, noting tier, justification, and initial strategic sufficiency targets.
3. **Map vulnerabilities** in Tier 1 and 2 sectors: supply chains, chokepoints, geographic and political risks.
4. **Design stress-test scenarios** that reflect plausible climate, cyber, and geopolitical shocks.
5. **Run stress-tests**, involving relevant ministries, regulators, firms, and, where appropriate, allied partners.
6. **Record failures and near-misses**, and revise the Essentiality Register, targets, and policy measures accordingly.
7. **Repeat regularly**, embedding learning into each cycle.

This loop is at the heart of RTT's approach to classification. It treats essentiality not as a fixed label, but as a working hypothesis that must be tested against reality.

8. Toolkit: Launching a Classification and Mapping Exercise

For a country or bloc beginning this work, a structured starting point is useful.

Toolkit 4 - First-Year Plan for Strategic Categorisation

- **Step 1: Mandate and team.**

  Establish a cross-ministerial taskforce under the Resilient Trade Authority with clear political backing and a one-year mandate to produce an initial Essentiality Register and vulnerability map.

- **Step 2: Criteria and tiers.**

  Agree on essentiality criteria and a tier structure (e.g., four tiers) and publish them as a short policy note.

- **Step 3: Draft register.**

  Populate a draft register of sectors and key goods, using expert input from line ministries, regulators, industry, and independent researchers.

- **Step 4: Rapid vulnerability scan.**

  For Tier 1 and 2 sectors, conduct an initial scan of key suppliers, routes, and chokepoints, using existing data where possible.

- **Step 5: Pilot stress-tests.**

  Run one or two table-top exercises on selected scenarios (for example, an export ban on a critical input and a river transport disruption) to test assumptions.

- **Step 6: Revise and publish.**

  Update the register and associated targets based on what the pilot tests reveal, and publish a public version with non-sensitive information.

- **Step 7: Set review cycle.**

  Commit to an annual review that updates classifications, incorporates new data, and expands stress-testing.

None of these steps requires perfection at the outset. The aim is to create a structured process that can improve over time, rather than waiting for complete information that never arrives.

9. Conclusion: Classification as the Spine of RTT

This chapter has argued that credible resilience begins with honest classification. Without a clear and dynamic understanding of which sectors are essential, policy cannot distinguish between areas where redundancy and allied interdependence are vital and areas where openness can remain unconstrained.

By defining criteria, building a tiered Essentiality Register, mapping vulnerabilities, and conducting interdependence stress-tests, states and blocs can turn abstract concerns about fragility into concrete design choices. The result is not a guarantee against disruption, but a more realistic allocation of attention and resources.

The next steps in RTT build directly on this spine. Once sectors are classified and vulnerabilities understood, governments can turn to **capacity-building** in essentials, **labour systems** that support resilience, and **governance structures** that hold the entire framework together. Those topics are the focus of the chapters that follow.

Endnotes

1. WTO. (2021). *World Trade Report 2021: Economic resilience and trade.* World Trade Organization.
2. OECD. (2021). *Bouncing back: Rebuilding resilient supply chains.* Organisation for Economic Co-operation and Development.
3. National Academies of Sciences, Engineering, and Medicine. (2022). *Building Resilient Supply Chains: A Strategy for Strengthening U.S. Resilience.*
4. IMF. (2023). *Geoeconomic fragmentation and the future of multilateralism.* International Monetary Fund.
5. European Commission. (2021–2023). Communications on *Open Strategic Autonomy* and updated industrial strategy.
6. World Bank. (2020). *Shock Waves II: Managing the Impact of Compound Shocks on Supply Chains.*

CHAPTER 5

THE ECONOMICS OF STRATEGIC CAPACITY

Resilient Trade Theory (RTT) is not a rejection of economics. It is an attempt to bring economic thinking into closer alignment with the world as it actually is: volatile, unequal, and strategically contested. The standard tools, prices, comparative advantage, welfare gains from trade, remain useful. They are simply incomplete when the risk of systemic disruption and political coercion is ignored.

This chapter looks at RTT through an economic lens. It asks three core questions:

1. How should we rethink **comparative advantage** when resilience and coercion risk matter?
2. What is the **investment logic** for strategic capacity in essential sectors, and how does it differ from short-term profitability?
3. How can we define and finance **strategic sufficiency** without sliding into costly self-sufficiency?

The aim is to show that building resilience in essentials is not anti-economic. It is a form of rational insurance against very large, very real risks that markets alone have not managed well.

1. What Standard Economics Gets Right, and What It Misses

Classical trade theory explains why countries specialise in what they can produce relatively efficiently and trade for the rest. This specialisation, under stable conditions and with well-functioning markets, increases overall welfare. The empirical record shows clear benefits from trade liberalisation in many settings: higher productivity, greater variety, and lower prices.[1]

RTT does not dispute those gains. But it points to three gaps in the conventional framework:

1. **Disruption externalities.**

   Standard models treat shocks as temporary and local. In reality, some shocks are systemic and propagate rapidly through supply chains, pandemics, cyberattacks, climate extremes, and export controls. The costs of these disruptions are not fully borne by the firms that choose lean, concentrated structures; they are borne by downstream sectors and households who had no say in that choice.

2. **Option value of capacity.**

   Maintaining domestic or allied capacity in essential sectors, even when it appears more expensive in normal times, has value as an option: it allows a country to respond when global flows falter or when political conditions change. That option value is under-priced when we focus narrowly on current average costs.

3. **Coercion risk.**

   Trade networks can be used as instruments of power. A country that controls critical inputs can influence the behaviour of others, not by setting tariffs but by threatening interruption. The welfare costs of being exposed to such leverage are real, but they do not appear directly in price comparisons.

These gaps mean that a purely efficiency-first strategy can generate hidden fragility. From an economic perspective, resilience investments in essential sectors can be thought of as **correcting three failures**: a risk externality, an under-valued option, and a neglected dimension of strategic risk.[2]

2. Rethinking Comparative Advantage Through a Resilience Lens

Comparative advantage, as usually taught, is a static concept. It compares opportunity costs across sectors at a point in time and concludes that both sides gain from specialisation and trade. In a world without major shocks, this is a useful approximation. In a world with recurrent systemic shocks and coercion, it is incomplete.

Two adjustments are needed.

Adjusting for Disruption

First, comparative advantage should be understood as **contingent on reliability**. A supplier with a slight cost advantage but high disruption risk may be less attractive, in welfare terms, than a slightly more expensive supplier whose deliveries are reliable. The same applies domestically: a very lean, centralised production system may be more efficient until a shock arrives, at which point the cost of outages overwhelms prior savings.[3]

In essential sectors, RTT therefore encourages policymakers to think in terms of **resilience-adjusted advantage**: cost comparisons that explicitly take into account:

- Probability and expected severity of disruption.
- Time needed to reroute or substitute.
- System-wide impacts when failure occurs.

This does not require detailed mathematical models to be useful. Even qualitative assessments, rating suppliers and structures on both cost and resilience, can lead to different policy choices.

Adjusting for Coercion

Second, comparative advantage has traditionally treated political conditions as fixed. In practice, political relationships change. A country that is cheap and reliable today may not be so in ten years if its strategic posture shifts. When essential sectors depend heavily on suppliers in jurisdictions with divergent interests, the **risk of coercion** becomes part of the economic calculation.

From a resilience perspective, the "cheapest" supplier is not necessarily the one with the lowest unit cost. It is the one with the best combination of:

- Cost.
- Reliability under stress.
- Alignment with long-term political interests.
- Willingness to enter into enforceable continuity commitments.

This is why RTT emphasises **friend-shoring** and **resilience blocs**. It is not protectionism by another name. It is an attempt to anchor comparative advantage in a political context that recognises coercion as a real risk.

3. What Prices Don't Show: Hidden Costs of Fragility

Market prices incorporate information about current supply and demand, costs, and expectations. They do not automatically incorporate the broader social cost of losing a critical input in a crisis.

Consider two examples:

- A country depends on a small number of foreign plants for high-voltage transformers. Import prices are low, and domestic manufacturing has atrophied. In normal times, this appears efficient. But if those plants are disrupted, replacement times may stretch into months or years. During that period, grid restoration will be delayed, and parts of the economy may operate under rolling blackouts.
- A health system sources a key active pharmaceutical ingredient (API) from a small set of factories abroad. The price is competitive. No serious disruptions have occurred in recent years. But when a pandemic hits, export controls or factory shutdowns cut off supply. The health system then faces shortages of a core medicine, with consequences far beyond the API's original price.

In both cases, the **true cost of the initial structure** includes:

- The expected cost of occasional severe disruption.
- The cost of emergency measures (alternative sourcing, rationing, political crisis management).
- The long-term cost of lost output and trust.

These costs are often **externalised**, borne by the public, not by the firms whose sourcing and investment decisions created the fragility. As a result, private optimisation may rationally choose structures that are socially risky.[4]

RTT suggests that essential sectors require **public correction of this bias**. That correction can take different forms: regulated capacity requirements, public stockpiles, procurement rules that reward resilience, or direct public investment in strategic capacity. The important point is that prices alone are not a sufficient guide.

4. Defining Strategic Capacity

Strategic capacity, in the RTT sense, is not about maximising output everywhere. It is about ensuring that **minimum critical capabilities** exist in essential sectors, either domestically or within reliable alliances, so that society can withstand plausible shocks.

Strategic capacity has several components:

- **Physical capacity:** Facilities, equipment, and stockpiles that can produce or deliver essential goods at required volumes under stress.
- **Human capacity:** Skilled workers and managers who can operate, repair, and adapt systems when conditions are difficult.
- **Institutional capacity:** Organisations and rules that can coordinate production, allocate scarce resources, and activate contingency plans.
- **Allied capacity:** Trusted partners who can provide surge support, alternative routes, or complementary capabilities when national systems are strained.

The key is not to build large surplus capacity in every sector, but to **identify where failure would be critical and where recovery would be slow**, and to ensure the existence of robust backstops in those areas.

A useful analogy is emergency services. No one expects fire brigades or ambulance systems to be "profitable" in narrow commercial terms. They exist because the cost of not having them when needed is far greater than the cost of maintaining them. Strategic capacity in essentials plays a similar role. It is part of the basic infrastructure of a functioning state.

5. The Investment Logic: Continuity vs. Short-Term Profit

Once strategic capacity is defined, the next question is how much to invest, and where. The core difference between a resilience-oriented approach and a narrow profit-oriented approach is the **time horizon and the objective function.**

Short-Term Profitability

Private firms primarily seek to maximise returns to shareholders or owners. In many sectors, this leads to efficient outcomes. But in essential sectors where:

- Demand spikes under crisis conditions.
- Revenues are partly regulated.
- Externalities are large.
- Coercion risks exist.

private incentives may not align with social objectives.

For example, maintaining an under-utilised backup plant, keeping additional inventory, or investing in localised tooling may make little sense commercially if demand is stable and global supply is trusted. Firms are unlikely to fund these measures alone, especially when competitors can undercut them by free-riding on fragility.

Continuity-Focused Investment

From the state's perspective, the objective is different: to minimise the probability and impact of catastrophic failure in essentials over a multi-decade horizon. That implies willingness to:

- Pay a **resilience premium**, a modest additional cost in normal times, in exchange for a significant reduction in the cost of extreme events.

- Accept that some assets will be under-used in everyday conditions but vital when needed.
- View certain forms of capacity as public goods rather than commercial products.

This is not an argument for unlimited spending. It is an argument for **explicit trade-offs**: identifying where a small increase in recurring cost can avert a much larger expected loss.[5]

In practice, the investment logic requires three steps:

1. **Identify critical failure modes** in Tier 1 and 2 sectors (using the classification and mapping work from Chapter 4).
2. **Estimate the consequences** of failure in each mode, not in precise monetary terms, but at least in relative order of magnitude.
3. **Compare options** for reducing risk, domestic capacity, allied arrangements, stockpiles, diversification, and choose combinations where the resilience gain justifies the cost.

Where markets cannot or will not provide these options on their own, public policy must shape or supplement them.

6. Financing and Incentivising Strategic Capacity

The economic question then becomes: how should strategic capacity be financed and incentivised, and by whom?

Several tools are available.

Public Investment

In some cases, direct state investment is the simplest approach: building and maintaining strategic reserves, establishing publicly owned facilities (for example, vaccine production or testing labs), or funding core infrastructure (such as grid-strengthening projects). This approach is appropriate where:

- The asset is clearly essential.
- The revenue model is uncertain.
- Coordination across many actors would be complex.

Regulated Private Investment

In other contexts, private firms can build and maintain capacity under regulatory frameworks that:

- Guarantee a regulated return on invested capital (as in many energy and utility sectors).
- Require minimum capacity or stock levels as part of operating licences.
- Allow cost recovery through tariffs or public payments.

This model uses regulation to align private incentives with resilience goals, recognising that pure competition may under-provide capacity in essentials.

Market-Shaping Instruments

Additional instruments can be used to encourage investment in strategic capacity where neither pure public provision nor traditional regulation is ideal:

- **Advance market commitments (AMCs):** Governments commit to purchase a certain volume of a critical good at a pre-agreed price if conditions trigger it (for example, vaccines or diagnostics).

- **Capacity payments or availability premia:** Firms receive payment not only for what they produce, but for being able to produce on short notice (as in some electricity markets).
- **Resilience bonds or blended finance:** Public and private actors co-finance projects that reduce systemic risk, with returns linked in part to avoided losses.[6]

The choice of tool depends on the sector, the fiscal position of the state, and the structure of the market. The underlying logic, however, is consistent: **where the benefits of resilience are widely shared and the costs of failure are high, public policy must underwrite or mandate strategic capacity.**

7. Strategic Sufficiency vs. Self-Sufficiency

RTT introduces the concept of **strategic sufficiency (SS)** to avoid a false choice between fragile openness and costly autarky.

Strategic sufficiency is the idea that, for each essential sector, there is a minimum level of secure capacity, domestic plus allied, that allows the system to withstand plausible shocks without catastrophic loss. It is defined not as 100 per cent internal production, but as a combination of:

- Domestic anchor capacity.
- Reliable allied capacity with enforceable continuity commitments.
- Stockpiles and substitution options sufficient to bridge temporary gaps.

Several indicators can be used to operationalise SS:

- **Minimum domestic share** of critical inputs or production capacity.
- **Maximum concentration** of imports from any single non-allied supplier.

- **Minimum days of stock** for key goods.
- **Maximum time-to-recover** for core infrastructure components (relative to time-to-survive).

These indicators need not be precise to be useful. Even setting approximate thresholds, "no more than X per cent of this input from any single non-allied source", can guide trade, procurement, and investment decisions.[7]

Self-sufficiency, by contrast, would imply meeting all needs domestically. For most countries, in most sectors, that is neither realistic nor desirable. Strategic sufficiency aims at **enough control and flexibility to prevent coercion and system collapse**, while still benefiting from trade and specialisation.

8. Sectoral and Regional Illustrations

The abstract logic of strategic capacity becomes clearer when anchored in concrete sectors.

Agriculture

In staple agriculture, strategic capacity may include maintaining:

- Domestic seed systems and agronomic expertise.
- The ability to produce or import fertilizers from diversified sources.
- Storage and transport infrastructure capable of absorbing climate shocks.
- Agreements with key trading partners for continuity of grain flows during stress.

Latin American producers, for example, play a central role in global grain markets. Their capacity and resilience have direct implications for food security in North Africa, the Middle East, and parts of Asia. Conversely, import-dependent states must think about diversified sourcing and local buffer stocks as part of their own strategic capacity.

Energy and Grids

Energy systems require specialised equipment, transformers, control systems, turbines, often produced in a limited number of factories. Here, strategic capacity can include:

- Domestic or allied production of critical components.
- Shared transformer reserves at regional level.
- Investments in grid flexibility and interconnection.
- Local skills in maintenance and repair.

In Europe, the experience of gas supply shocks has already prompted moves towards diversified suppliers, shared storage, and coordinated demand management, elements of strategic capacity in action.

Technology and Digital Infrastructure

Semiconductors, cloud services, and digital backbones underpin many essential functions. Strategic capacity in this domain may include:

- Domestic design or manufacturing capabilities at key nodes.
- Trusted allied access to advanced chips.
- National or regional cloud infrastructure for critical public services.
- Strong cybersecurity and incident response capabilities.

East Asia and the United States are currently central to semiconductor supply chains. For many other regions, resilience will involve a mix of allied arrangements, domestic niche capabilities, and careful diversification of suppliers.

Military and Dual-use Sectors

Some capabilities have both civilian and defence relevance: satellite systems, secure communications, logistics networks, advanced manufacturing. Strategic capacity here supports not only economic resilience but national security. This is one area where many states already accept that pure efficiency is not sufficient; RTT extends that reasoning to a broader set of essential sectors.

9. Toolkit: Economic Questions for Strategic Capacity Decisions

To bring these ideas into day-to-day policy work, a practical checklist helps.

Toolkit 5 - Economic Questions for Strategic Capacity

1. **What happens if this sector fails?**

   Identify concrete consequences for lives, output, and social stability. If failure is tolerable, strategic capacity may not be needed.

2. **How long until alternatives can be activated?**

   Estimate time-to-recover (TTR) for domestic and allied options. Compare it to how long society can function without the sector (time-to-survive).

3. **Who currently decides the structure of this sector?**

   Are key decisions driven solely by private firms optimising for cost, or is there a public framework that reflects resilience needs?

4. **Where are the concentration risks?**

   Look at supplier concentration, geographic clustering, and dependency on specific jurisdictions.

5. **What is the cheapest way to reduce the worst risks?**

   Compare options: modest stockpiles, a small domestic facility, a continuity clause with an ally, or diversified sourcing.

6. **Who should pay for the capacity?**

   Decide whether costs should fall on taxpayers, consumers, or specific industries, and choose instruments accordingly (public investment, regulation, AMCs, capacity payments).

7. **How will we review and adjust?**

   Set a schedule and criteria for revisiting strategic capacity decisions as technologies and risks change.

These questions do not replace detailed analysis. They ensure that analysis is pointed at the right issues.

10. Conclusion: Economics in Service of Resilience

Resilient Trade Theory does not ask economists to abandon their tools. It asks them to use those tools in a way that reflects the realities of systemic risk and political contestation. The core claims of this chapter are simple:

- Comparative advantage must be understood in resilience-adjusted terms for essential sectors.
- Prices alone do not capture disruption externalities, option value, and coercion risk.
- Strategic capacity is a legitimate object of public policy where failure would be catastrophic and private incentives under-provide robustness.
- Strategic sufficiency offers a middle path between fragile dependence and costly self-sufficiency.

In the chapters that follow, these economic foundations are linked to concrete levers: labour systems, governance structures, and trade instruments. If we get the economics wrong, resilience will either be underbuilt or built in ways that are unnecessarily expensive. If we get it right, strategic capacity becomes what it should be: a measured, deliberate investment in the ability of societies to endure.

Endnotes

1. WTO. (2021). *World Trade Report 2021: Economic resilience and trade.* World Trade Organization.
2. IMF. (2023). *Geoeconomic fragmentation and the future of multilateralism.* International Monetary Fund.
3. Baldwin, R. (2016). *The Great Convergence: Information Technology and the New Globalization.* Harvard University Press.
4. OECD. (2021). *Bouncing back: Rebuilding resilient supply chains.* Organisation for Economic Co-operation and Development.
5. National Academies of Sciences, Engineering, and Medicine. (2022). *Building Resilient Supply Chains: A Strategy for Strengthening U.S. Resilience.*
6. Kremer, M., Levin, J., & Snyder, C. (2022). Designing advance market commitments for new vaccines. *Journal of Economic Perspectives, 36*(2), 55–78.
7. European Commission. (2021–2023). Communications on *Open Strategic Autonomy* and updated industrial and critical raw materials strategies.

CHAPTER 6

LABOUR SYSTEMS AS A CORE RESILIENCE ASSET

Resilient Trade Theory (RTT) treats labour as more than an input cost. It treats people, their skills, security, and willingness to show up under pressure, as a central component of national resilience.

When we talk about keeping food systems functioning, power grids stable, hospitals open, logistics moving, and digital infrastructure secure, it is easy to focus on infrastructure and technology. Yet in every essential sector, continuity ultimately depends on workers: farmers and technicians, nurses and engineers, drivers and dispatchers, grid operators and cybersecurity teams. If these people are underpaid, exhausted, precarious, or simply absent, resilience plans will not survive first contact with reality.

This chapter develops the labour dimension of RTT. It argues that essential sectors require a **minimum liveable wage**, credible **training pathways** aligned with national strategic objectives, and **regional rebalancing** that anchors resilience in places often left behind by globalisation. The point is straightforward: a state that expects continuity from its essential sectors must offer continuity to the people who sustain them.

1. Why Labour Belongs at the Centre of Resilience

Resilience debates often start with hardware: warehouses, stockpiles, ports, plants, pipelines, data centres. But hardware does nothing on its own. It must be designed, operated, maintained, repaired, and adapted. In practice, three labour-related realities shape resilience outcomes.

The Human Bottleneck

In many countries, essential sectors face chronic labour shortages. Utilities struggle to recruit and retain line workers and control-room operators. Hospitals depend on overstretched nurses and support staff. Agricultural workforces are ageing, with too few younger workers entering the field. Logistics firms report persistent vacancies for drivers and technicians.[1]

When shocks occur, these shortages become acute. Extended shifts, heightened risk, and social pressures all fall on a workforce that is already thin. The result can be cascading failure: not because the physical system is inherently weak, but because there are not enough people to keep it running.

The Incentive Problem

If essential-sector jobs are low-paid, precarious, or socially undervalued, people will leave when alternatives appear. The most capable and mobile will depart first. This is rational behaviour at the individual level, but collectively it erodes the pool of experienced workers that resilience requires.

The incentives are particularly misaligned when essential roles have high responsibility and high stress, but wages and conditions do not reflect that reality. At that point, resilience becomes dependent on a sense of vocational duty that may not survive repeated crises.

The Trust Link

Resilience is also a matter of social trust. Populations are more likely to accept emergency measures, rationing, priority lanes, temporary restrictions, if they believe that essential workers are being treated fairly and that burdens are shared. Conversely, if they perceive that those keeping systems running are underpaid while others profit from the crisis, legitimacy can erode quickly.[2]

RTT therefore places labour systems at the core of its design. It treats **minimum liveable wages, skills pipelines**, and **regional inclusion** as resilience instruments, not as optional social add-ons.

2. The Minimum Liveable Wage in Essential Sectors

A central proposal in RTT is that essential sectors should be underpinned by a **minimum liveable wage (MLW)**, a wage floor set not only with reference to subsistence, but with reference to the dignity and responsibility of the work.

Why a Liveable Wage, not just a Minimum Wage

Standard minimum wages are typically designed to prevent extreme exploitation. They may be set low, eroded by inflation, or ignored in practice. A **liveable wage**, by contrast, is anchored in what is required for a worker and their household to meet basic needs, participate in society, and sustain their role over time.[3] For resilience purposes, this matters because:

- Workers in essential sectors are expected to be present during crises, often at personal risk.
- Their ability to absorb shocks, childcare disruptions, temporary illness, increased transport costs, depends on financial stability.

- Chronic financial stress undermines attention, decision-making, and health, all of which are crucial in high-stakes roles.

Setting an MLW in essential sectors signals that the state recognises their strategic importance. It reduces turnover, supports skills retention, and creates a base from which additional expectations (such as extra shifts during emergencies) can credibly be made.

Scope and Calibration

An MLW approach does not require that every job in the economy immediately meet a new standard. RTT focuses on **Tier 1 and Tier 2 sectors** (as defined in Chapter 4): those whose failure would rapidly compromise basic welfare or critical systems.

Within those sectors, an MLW can be calibrated to:

- Local cost of living, with periodic updates.
- Sector-specific stressors (for example, shift work, high-risk environments).
- The need to attract and retain workers with specific skills.

This is not purely a wage policy. It can be complemented by:

- Predictable scheduling or fair shift premiums.
- Access to childcare and eldercare.
- Health and mental health support.
- Paid training and progression pathways.

The combination of MLW and conditions creates **resilience-compatible jobs**, roles that can realistically be filled and sustained over the long term.

Economic and Political Considerations

Critics may argue that higher wages in essential sectors will increase costs for consumers or strain public budgets. RTT offers three responses:

1. A modest increase in essential-sector wages is a small price compared to the economic and social cost of system failures.
2. MLW in essentials can be financed partly through efficiency gains elsewhere, progressive taxation, or targeted subsidies that avoid blunt price increases.
3. Politically, a clear narrative, linking MLW to national security and continuity, can help build support for such measures.[4]

In short, a society that expects essential workers to stay when others can leave must ensure that those workers can live decently.

3. Workforce Training Aligned with Strategic Objectives

Wages and conditions keep people in essential sectors. Training and education ensure that they have the skills required for resilience.

Skills as Strategic Capacity

Chapter 5 introduced the concept of **strategic capacity**. Skills are a central part of that capacity. Without enough people who can install and maintain transformers, operate grid control systems, manage water treatment plants, produce and test vaccines, or secure digital infrastructure, physical investments cannot deliver resilience.[5]

RTT encourages states to treat training in essential sectors as a **strategic programme**, not a marginal component of education policy.

Key elements include:

- **Sector-specific pipelines.** Technical and vocational programmes in fields such as power systems, logistics, agricultural science, water engineering, biomedical manufacturing, and cybersecurity.
- **Mid-career pathways.** Routes for workers in adjacent fields to re-skill into essential sectors, supported by stipends or employer partnerships.
- **Apprenticeships and dual systems.** Combining classroom learning with supervised practical work, particularly in infrastructure and manufacturing roles.

Aligning Training with Classification

The Essentiality Register described in Chapter 4 provides a natural anchor for training policy. For each Tier 1 and 2 sector, policymakers can ask:

- What core occupations are needed to sustain and repair this system?
- What is the current age profile and vacancy rate in these occupations?
- How many trainees and apprentices are being prepared each year?
- Are there geographic gaps where local capacity is thin?

Answers to these questions can guide:

- Expansion or redirection of vocational programmes.
- Scholarships or stipends for students entering essential fields.
- Regional training centres linked to specific infrastructure (for example, ports, energy hubs, agricultural regions).

In East Asia, for example, national strategies around electronics and advanced manufacturing have been supported by deliberate investments in engineering and technical education. In the Nordic countries, energy and maritime sectors have long-established vocational pathways. RTT suggests extending this logic to a broader set of essential sectors.

International Dimensions

Skills do not stop at borders. For some countries, especially small states or those with ageing populations, resilience will depend partly on **labour mobility arrangements** with trusted partners:

- Mutual recognition of qualifications in essential occupations.
- Fast-track visa schemes for critical workers, triggered by specific shocks.
- Joint training programmes or campus exchanges focused on resilience-related skills.

These arrangements must be carefully designed to avoid stripping poorer countries of their own essential personnel. Well-structured agreements can include return pathways, training of additional workers, or financial support for sending-country training systems.[6]

4. Regional Rebalancing Through Labour Equity

Resilience is spatial as well as functional. Essential sectors are physically located in specific places: ports, pipelines, grain belts, energy corridors, data centres. Many of these are outside major metropolitan areas. Yet globalisation has often concentrated high-value employment and investment in large cities, leaving other regions behind.

RTT argues that **regional labour equity** is both a justice concern and a resilience opportunity.

The Regional Mismatch

In many countries:

- Rural and smaller urban regions host key infrastructure, ports, refineries, transmission lines, water reservoirs, agricultural land, but have limited access to stable, well-paid jobs outside a narrow set of activities.
- Youth migrate to large cities or abroad, leaving aging populations and thin local labour pools;
- Local economies become vulnerable to a small number of employers or sectors.

This pattern weakens resilience by:

- Reducing the number of people available to operate and maintain essential infrastructure locally.
- Increasing the risk that local discontent will translate into resistance to infrastructure projects.
- Making it harder to mobilise community-level support during crises.

Using Resilience Investments to Rebalance

Resilience-oriented investment, stockpiles, local processing, storage facilities, maintenance hubs, training centres, can be deliberately sited in regions that have historically been under-served. This can:

- Create stable employment linked to essential sectors.
- Anchor skills and institutions in places that host critical infrastructure.
- Strengthen local support for resilience measures.

Examples might include:

- Locating new grain storage and processing facilities in secondary cities along key transport corridors.
- Building regional maintenance centres for grid equipment or railway rolling stock.
- Establishing vaccine fill-and-finish plants in regions with good logistics but limited industry.
- Creating training academies for water and sanitation technicians in riverine or coastal areas.

These investments should be paired with MLW and training pathways, so that new jobs are both decent and accessible to local populations.

Social Cohesion and Risk Management

Regional labour equity has an additional resilience benefit: **it strengthens social cohesion.** When communities see that national resilience strategies include them, through jobs, institutions, and visible infrastructure, they are more likely to cooperate with emergency plans, support allied partnerships, and resist divisive narratives.

Conversely, if resilience investments are perceived as benefiting only core metropolitan regions while rural or peripheral areas bear the environmental or social costs, trust will erode. That erosion becomes a risk factor in itself, especially in times of crisis.

5. Exhibit: Essential Sectors and Labour Fragility

A simple way to visualise the labour dimension is to map essential sectors against two variables: **wage adequacy** and **skills pipeline strength.**

Exhibit 1 - Labour Fragility in Essential Sectors (Conceptual)

- **Quadrant I (High wage, strong pipeline):**

  Some specialised medical professions; certain high-skill energy and technology roles in advanced economies. Resilience risk is relatively low on the labour side.

- **Quadrant II (Low wage, strong pipeline):**

  Roles where cultural or vocational norms still attract entrants despite low pay, but pressure is building (for example, some nursing and teaching contexts). Risk of future attrition is high.

- **Quadrant III (Low wage, weak pipeline):**

  Agricultural labour, frontline logistics, some care roles, maintenance trades in neglected regions. This is the critical quadrant for resilience: systems depend heavily on workers who are underpaid and not being replaced.

- **Quadrant IV (High wage, weak pipeline):**

  Niche technical roles where pay is substantial but training capacity is limited and entry barriers are high (for example, certain cybersecurity or advanced engineering specialties). Vulnerability arises from small absolute numbers rather than low pay.

RTT focuses particularly on Quadrant III. Without intervention, MLW, training, and regional investment—these sectors are likely to become chronic bottlenecks in any resilience strategy.

6. International Examples and Lessons

While RTT is a forward-looking framework, it can draw on existing practices.

Japan and Skilled Trades

Japan's emphasis on manufacturing excellence has historically been supported by vocational schools and firm-based training. In sectors such as automotive and machinery, this has created deep pools of skilled workers who sustain quality and continuity. However, demographic ageing now pressures this model. The lesson for RTT is clear: **robust training systems must be maintained and renewed**, not assumed to be self-sustaining.

Nordic Countries and Essential Services

Northern European states have combined relatively high wages and strong social protections with high expectations for public service performance. Health, education, and energy systems benefit from a steady supply of trained personnel and a degree of social prestige. This does not eliminate pressure or shortages, but it reduces turnover and helps sustain continuity.[7]

Southeast Asia and Logistics Labour

Ports and logistics hubs in Southeast Asia have become central to global trade. In many cases, operational excellence rests on large, skilled workforces who manage high volumes under tight schedules. Yet some segments of this labour, especially subcontracted or informal workers, remain vulnerable. Here, RTT would argue for **formalisation, wage floors, and training** as part of any resilience strategy that relies on these corridors.

Latin America and Agricultural Workers

Agricultural exports from Latin America underpin food security in many importing regions. Yet many agricultural workers themselves remain in precarious conditions. A resilience lens suggests that **securing the rights, incomes, and skills of these workers is part of global food system stability**, not simply a domestic social policy.

These examples point in one direction: where labour in essential sectors is treated as expendable, resilience is thin. Where it is recognised and supported, resilience is thicker, even if other vulnerabilities remain.

7. Toolkit: Labour Policy for Resilient Trade

Turning these ideas into policy requires concrete steps.

Toolkit 6 - Labour System Checks for Essential Sectors

1. **Map essential occupations.**

   For each Tier 1 and 2 sector, list the key occupations without which the system cannot function (for example, ICU nurses, substation technicians, water plant operators, long-haul drivers, warehouse supervisors, cybersecurity analysts).

2. **Assess wage adequacy.**

   Compare current wages and conditions for these occupations to a liveable wage benchmark. Identify gaps and regions where they are most severe.

3. **Analyse age and vacancy profiles.**

   Determine the age distribution, vacancy rate, and projected retirements over the next 5–10 years. Highlight occupations at risk of depletion.

4. **Review training pathways.**

   Identify existing vocational and higher education programmes supplying these roles. Assess throughput, dropout rates, and geographic coverage.

5. **Design MLW and support packages.**

   Set a minimum liveable wage for essential occupations, paired with measures such as predictable scheduling, childcare support, and funded training.

6. **Plan regional investment.**

   Align new resilience projects, storage, maintenance hubs, training centres, with regions that host critical infrastructure but lack stable, well-paid employment.

7. **Monitor and adjust.**

   Track turnover, vacancy rates, and training completion annually. Treat rising vacancies in essential roles as resilience warnings, not just labour market facts.

These steps will not turn labour systems around overnight. But they create a structure for gradual, deliberate alignment of labour policy with resilience goals.

8. Conclusion: People as the First Line of Defence

It is tempting to think of resilience as a matter of infrastructure and technology. In reality, the first line of defence is always people: those who plant crops and repair engines, who staff emergency rooms and dispatch centres, who read fault codes and climb towers in storms.

Resilient Trade Theory insists that any serious attempt to secure essential sectors must begin with them. That means:

- Paying wages that reflect the responsibility we ask them to carry.
- Providing training pathways that create depth, not just minimal coverage.
- Investing in regions whose people and infrastructure we rely on but too often neglect.

Labour systems are not a peripheral chapter in RTT. They are its backbone. Without a stable, skilled, and respected workforce in essential sectors, stockpiles will sit unused, plans will remain on paper, and alliances will have nothing solid to rest on.

The next chapters turn to the institutional and governance structures that can hold this entire framework together: the bodies that classify sectors, coordinate policy, oversee stress-tests, and ensure that resilience remains a living practice rather than a one-off initiative. But those structures will only succeed if they recognise what this chapter has argued: **people are not a line item in resilience, they are the system.**

Endnotes

1. OECD. (2021). *Bouncing back: Rebuilding resilient supply chains.* Organisation for Economic Co-operation and Development.
2. Norris, F. H., Stevens, S. P., Pfefferbaum, B., Wyche, K. F., & Pfefferbaum, R. L. (2008). Community resilience as a metaphor, theory, set of capacities, and strategy for disaster readiness. *American Journal of Community Psychology, 41*(1–2), 127–150.

3. Anker, R., & Anker, M. (2017). *Living Wages Around the World: Manual for Measurement.* Edward Elgar.
4. ILO. (2022). *World Employment and Social Outlook 2022: The role of labour in building resilient economies.* International Labour Organization.
5. National Academies of Sciences, Engineering, and Medicine. (2022). *Building Resilient Supply Chains: A Strategy for Strengthening U.S. Resilience.*
6. Clemens, M., & Pritchett, L. (2019). The new economic case for migration restrictions: An assessment. *Journal of Economic Perspectives, 33*(1), 141–164.
7. Esping-Andersen, G. (2015). *Welfare states and the distribution of life chances.* European Review, 23(S1), S25–S40.

CHAPTER 7

INSTITUTIONAL DESIGN FOR RESILIENCE GOVERNANCE

Even the best ideas fail without institutions capable of carrying them. Resilient Trade Theory (RTT) is no exception. Strategic categorisation, capacity-building, labour policy, and differentiated trade rules all depend on something simple but often missing: a place in the state where these issues are held together, monitored over time, and adjusted as reality changes.

Resilience cannot be run as a side project. It cannot live only in strategy papers, ad hoc crisis committees, or individual ministries. It needs **governance**, clear mandates, defined responsibilities, and routines that survive electoral cycles and shifts in political attention.

This chapter focuses on institutional design. It asks how a country or bloc can build governance structures that:

- Anchor RTT in day-to-day policy.
- Coordinate across ministries and levels of government.
- Run audits, simulations, and stress-tests.
- Communicate risks and trade-offs transparently.
- Adapt to changing technology, climate, and geopolitics.
- Avoid becoming captured, politicised, or ceremonial.

The core proposal is the creation of a **Resilient Trade Authority (RTA)** or equivalent body, supported by a network of line ministries, regulators, and external partners. The details will differ across political systems, but the underlying design principles are widely applicable.

1. Why Governance Is a Precondition for Implementation

Resilience, as treated in earlier chapters, is not a single policy. It is a **system of decisions**: how we classify sectors, where we build capacity, which trade agreements we sign, how we treat workers in essentials, and how we design corridors with allies. Without coherent governance, these decisions are likely to be:

- Fragmented: each ministry pursues its own priorities, with limited awareness of cross-sectoral impacts.
- Reactive: measures are adopted after crises, fade once memory recedes, and are rarely evaluated.
- Vulnerable to capture: powerful sectors frame their own interests as "strategic" and secure special treatment without scrutiny.
- Inconsistent over time: changes in government reverse or freeze previous measures, leaving systems half-built.

Institutional design is the way to protect RTT from these predictable failures. It creates **structures that remember** when individuals and cabinets change. It embeds routines, audits, simulations, public reporting, that force attention back onto resilience even when the news cycle is quiet.[1]

Without such structures, resilience remains a set of good intentions. With them, it can become a steady, if imperfect, practice.

2. The Case for a Resilient Trade Authority (RTA)

At the centre of RTT governance is the proposal to establish a **Resilient Trade Authority**, an institution responsible for integrating resilience into trade, industrial, and security policy.

Core Mandate

An RTA's mandate should include at least six functions:

1. **Maintain the Essentiality Register.**

   Lead the classification of sectors and critical goods, ensure regular reviews, and document justifications for tier assignments and changes.

2. **Map vulnerabilities and chokepoints.**

   Coordinate cross-sectoral analyses of supply chains, infrastructure, and labour risks in Tier 1 and 2 sectors.

3. **Design and run stress-tests.**

   Develop scenarios, organise exercises, and produce structured lessons for domestic and allied resilience.

4. **Advise on trade and procurement.**

   Review trade agreements, procurement rules, and investment policies for consistency with resilience objectives; propose resilience clauses and continuity mechanisms.

5. **Monitor resilience indicators.**

   Develop metrics—stock levels, supplier concentration, outage days, labour vacancies, and report on them publicly.

6. **Convene and coordinate.**

   Bring together ministries, regulators, and external stakeholders to align decisions that affect essential sectors.

The RTA is not intended to replace line ministries. It is intended to **see across them**, ensure that resilience is not lost in sectoral silos, and provide structured advice to political leaders.

Institutional Form

In practice, an RTA might take different forms:

- A standalone agency with statutory independence, similar to a central bank or competition authority in some systems.
- A powerful unit within a central ministry (for example, economics, finance, or prime minister's office) with clear cross-cutting authority.
- A hybrid structure, combining a small central team with embedded resilience units in key ministries.

The exact form matters less than the **combination of authority and insulation**:

- Enough authority to request data, convene actors, and influence decisions.
- Enough insulation from day-to-day political conflict to maintain continuity and long-term focus.[2]

3. Anatomy of an Effective RTA

Designing an RTA is not only about mandate; it is also about internal structure.

Skills and Composition

An effective RTA needs:

- **Economic and trade expertise** to understand how supply chains, prices, and agreements work in practice.
- **Sectoral knowledge** in agriculture, energy, health, digital, logistics, and defence-related industries.

- **Risk and systems analysis** capacity to run scenario planning, stress-tests, and network mapping.
- **Legal and diplomatic skills** to translate resilience concerns into treaty language and procurement frameworks.
- **Data and analytics** capabilities to manage indicators and early-warning systems.

This does not mean the RTA must be large. It means it must be **interdisciplinary**, and able to draw on external expertise where necessary, including universities, think-tanks, and industry bodies.

Position in the Decision Chain

The RTA should have a clear route into political decision-making:

- Regular reporting to a cabinet-level committee on economic and security affairs.
- Formal consultation rights on major trade agreements, critical infrastructure decisions, and industrial strategies.
- The ability to publish independent assessments, subject to confidentiality rules, when resilience concerns are significant.

The aim is not to give the RTA veto power over all decisions, but to ensure that resilience is **consistently represented** in deliberations.

Interaction with Line Ministries

Resilience is inherently cross-cutting. The RTA's work must therefore be embedded within a **network of ministry focal points**:

- Each key ministry (trade, agriculture, energy, health, transport, digital, defence, labour) designates a resilience lead.

- These leads participate in regular coordination meetings chaired by the RTA.
- Joint working groups tackle specific issues, such as a critical input, corridor, or sector, bringing together all relevant actors.

This structure reduces the risk of duplication or conflict. It also helps translate RTA recommendations into concrete, sector-specific policies.

4. Audits, Simulations, and the Discipline of Routine

Resilience without measurement and rehearsal is a slogan. RTT's institutional design therefore places **audits and simulations** at the heart of governance.

Resilience Audits

A resilience audit is a structured review of how well a sector or system can cope with specified shocks. Unlike financial audits, which look backward, resilience audits look forward, asking "what if" questions and assessing preparedness.

Key features include:

- **Scope:** Focus on Tier 1 and 2 sectors, and on cross-cutting systems such as logistics and digital infrastructure.
- **Method:** Combine quantitative indicators (stock levels, supplier concentration, TTR) with qualitative assessments (governance quality, local capacity).
- **Frequency:** Conduct full audits on a multi-year cycle (for example, every three years), with annual updates on key metrics.[3]

Audits should result in:

- A set of **findings**, where capacity is adequate, borderline, or deficient.
- A set of **recommendations**, changes in investment, regulation, trade arrangements, or labour policies.
- A public **summary**, sufficient to inform citizens without exposing sensitive details.

Simulations and Stress-tests

Simulations complement audits by **testing systems under pressure**. They might involve:

- Table-top exercises with ministers and senior officials.
- Sector-specific drills involving operators, emergency services, and firms.
- Cross-border simulations with allied partners.

For example:

- A simulation of a large-scale cyberattack on port systems, combined with a severe storm, to test alternative logistics plans.
- A scenario in which a key exporting country imposes export controls on a critical input, to test procurement, rationing, and substitution mechanisms.
- A drill where energy infrastructure failures occur during a heat wave, to assess health system and grid responses.

An effective RTA:

- Designs these scenarios.
- Coordinates participants.
- Captures lessons.
- Ensures that follow-up actions are tracked.

International experience shows that such exercises, when taken seriously, can reveal vulnerabilities that routine analysis misses.[4]

5. Cross-Ministerial Coordination and the Problem of Silos

Resilience governance fails quickly when ministries act alone. Trade agreements negotiated without input from energy or health ministries may expose critical sectors to risk. Industrial policies may support capacity that undermines environmental or social objectives. Labour policies may ignore the specific needs of essential sectors.

The RTA's coordinating role therefore requires **formal mechanisms** to break silos.

Cabinet Committees and Joint Mandates

A simple but powerful step is to create a **cabinet-level committee** responsible for economic and resilience affairs, with membership drawn from:

- Finance and economy.
- Trade and foreign affairs.
- Agriculture, energy, health, transport, digital.
- Defence and interior.
- Labour and social affairs.

This committee:

- Receives RTA reports.
- Approves the Essentiality Register and major resilience strategies.
- Arbitrates trade-offs between sectors when necessary.

Below cabinet level, **joint mandates** can be created for specific tasks. For example:

- A joint trade-health mandate for negotiating medical supply continuity clauses.
- A joint energy-transport-environment mandate for corridor planning.
- A joint labour-industry mandate for essential-sector training programmes.

These joint mandates make it harder for any single ministry to ignore resilience concerns that fall outside its traditional remit.

Data Sharing and Confidentiality

Effective coordination requires **data flows**. Ministries and regulators must be willing to share information on utilisation, capacity, incidents, and vulnerabilities. At the same time, sensitive data, commercial or security-related, must be protected.

An RTA can help by:

- Establishing standardised reporting formats for resilience indicators.
- Creating secure platforms for data sharing.
- Setting protocols for classification, access, and publication.

International organisations have begun to explore similar challenges in the context of pandemic preparedness, cyber incidents, and climate risk.[5] RTT extends those efforts to the broader field of trade-related resilience.

6. Avoiding Politicisation and Institutional Capture

Any powerful institution runs the risk of politicisation or capture. An RTA could be used to reward favoured sectors with "strategic" status, shelter firms from competition, or justify ideologically motivated isolation. It could also become paralysed by partisan conflict or sidelined when its findings are inconvenient.

RTT therefore emphasises **safeguards**.

Legal and Procedural Safeguards

Several measures can help:

- **Statutory mandate.** Anchor the RTA's existence and core functions in law, with clear objectives focused on resilience in defined essential sectors.
- **Transparent criteria.** Publish essentiality criteria, resilience indicators, and stress-testing methodologies to reduce arbitrary decision-making.
- **Reporting requirements.** Require regular public reports, with explanations for major decisions and changes in classification.
- **Review mechanisms.** Allow external bodies, a parliamentary committee, auditor general, or independent panel, to review the RTA's work.

These mechanisms do not eliminate politics, but they make it harder to hide decisions that deviate sharply from stated principles.

Composition and Appointments

The composition of the RTA's leadership matters for credibility. Options include:

- Mixed boards combining government officials, independent experts, and representatives from social partners.
- Fixed-term appointments with staggered terms to reduce vulnerability to single-election swings.
- Appointment processes that include parliamentary confirmation or public hearings.

Diversity of background, sectoral, regional, and disciplinary, can also reduce groupthink and the risk of capture by a single interest.

Policy Guardrails

Finally, policy design itself can provide guardrails:

- Use **sunset clauses** for protective measures, requiring renewal based on evidence rather than inertia.
- Tie certain interventions to **objective triggers** (for example, supplier concentration or outage thresholds) rather than discretionary decisions.
- Limit the scope of "strategic" designations to Tier 1 and 2 sectors defined through a structured process.

These guardrails allow resilience policy to be robust without becoming a blanket excuse for opportunistic protectionism.[6]

7. Inclusive and Participatory Governance

Resilience is not only a technical and political issue; it is a social one. Institutions that design and oversee resilience policy will be more legitimate, and more effective, if they incorporate input from those affected by their decisions.

Stakeholder Councils

An RTA can be supported by **stakeholder councils** that include:

- Industry associations from essential sectors.
- Trade unions and worker representatives.
- Civil society organisations concerned with equity, environment, and human rights.
- Academic and technical experts.
- Local government representatives from regions that host critical infrastructure.

These councils:

- Comment on the Essentiality Register and resilience strategies.
- Provide ground-level feedback on labour conditions, operational realities, and public communication.
- Help identify unintended consequences of proposed measures.

Their role is advisory, not executive, but their presence helps prevent blind spots.

Local and Regional Involvement

Because many resilience measures are implemented locally, stockpiles, infrastructure, evacuation and rationing plans, local governments need a voice in governance. They can:

- Inform national authorities about local vulnerabilities and capacities.
- Help prioritise investments.
- Coordinate community-level preparedness.

RTT encourages **multilevel governance**, where national strategies are adapted to local realities rather than imposed uniformly from the centre.

8. Toolkit: Designing a Resilient Trade Authority

For governments considering the creation or reform of resilience governance structures, a practical starting outline is useful.

Toolkit 7 - Steps to Design and Launch an RTA

1. **Define the mandate.**

   Specify which sectors and functions the RTA will cover (for example, Tier 1 and 2 sectors, cross-cutting infrastructure, and related trade and labour policies).

2. **Choose the institutional form.**

   Decide whether the RTA will be a standalone agency, a unit in a central ministry, or a hybrid. Ensure it has both authority and some independence.

3. **Map interfaces.**

   Identify the ministries, regulators, and external bodies with which the RTA must interact. Define focal points and communication channels.

4. **Set core processes.**

   Establish processes for maintaining the Essentiality Register, conducting audits, running simulations, and producing public reports.

5. **Build the team.**

   Recruit staff with a mix of economic, sectoral, risk, legal, and data skills. Where gaps exist, plan partnerships with universities and think-tanks.

6. **Create safeguards.**

   Embed transparency, review, and sunset mechanisms in the RTA's statutes or operating rules. Publish criteria and methodologies.

7. **Pilot and iterate.**

   Begin with a limited set of sectors and scenarios. Learn from early audits and exercises. Adjust structures and processes based on experience.

The goal is not to design a perfect institution on paper, but to **create a capable starting point** that can evolve.

9. Conclusion: Institutions That Remember and Learn

Resilient Trade Theory depends on more than insight. It depends on institutions that can **remember** lessons from past shocks, **coordinate** across sectors, and **learn** from stress-tests and near misses.

A Resilient Trade Authority, appropriately designed, empowered, and constrained, provides a place in the state where this work can live. It does not replace politics, but it can help ensure that political choices are made with a clear view of vulnerabilities and options. It does not eliminate risk, but it can make risk visible and manageable rather than hidden and explosive.

Without such institutions, RTT risks being absorbed into familiar cycles: concern after crisis, neglect in quiet times, and repeated surprise when systems fail again. With them, there is at least a chance that resilience can move from rhetoric to routine.

The next part of this book turns from design to practice: how to build domestic capacity, craft differentiated trade policy, and support social cohesion so that the governance structures described here have something solid to work with.

Endnotes

1. WTO. (2021). *World Trade Report 2021: Economic resilience and trade.* World Trade Organization.
2. IMF. (2023). *Geoeconomic fragmentation and the future of multilateralism.* International Monetary Fund.
3. National Academies of Sciences, Engineering, and Medicine. (2022). *Building Resilient Supply Chains: A Strategy for Strengthening U.S. Resilience.*
4. OECD. (2021). *Bouncing back: Rebuilding resilient supply chains.* Organisation for Economic Co-operation and Development.
5. WHO. (2022). *Strengthening pandemic preparedness: Simulation exercises and stress tests.* World Health Organization.
6. Rodrik, D. (2018). What do trade agreements really do? *Journal of Economic Perspectives, 32*(2), 73–90.

PART III

The Resilient Trade Model in Practice

CHAPTER 8

DOMESTIC CAPACITY BUILDING

Resilient Trade Theory (RTT) only becomes real when it touches factories, fields, ports, warehouses, labs, and classrooms. Classification, governance, and strategy are necessary, but they are not sufficient. At some point, a country that wants to be resilient must be able to say: *we can actually produce, store, move, repair, and staff the things that keep us alive and functioning.*

That is what **domestic capacity building** is about. It is not an argument for doing everything at home. It is an argument for making sure that, in essential sectors, there is enough capability, domestic and allied, to keep systems running when global flows falter.

This chapter focuses on the "how." It looks at:

- Public investment and incentive design for critical infrastructure.
- Strategic reserves and localised production nodes.
- Human capital and institutional depth.
- Education policy aligned with resilience rather than just generic growth.

The goal is practical: to outline what it means, in concrete terms, to build capacity that supports resilience instead of assuming it.

1. From Strategy to Concrete Assets

Previous chapters have argued that essential sectors must be identified (Chapter 4), supported by strategic capacity (Chapter 5), and staffed by a resilient workforce (Chapter 6). Domestic capacity building is where those strands meet in physical and institutional form.

In RTT terms, domestic capacity building means:

- **Creating and maintaining assets**, plants, depots, data centres, labs, training facilities, that can operate under stress.
- **Distributing those assets** in ways that reduce single points of failure.
- **Ensuring that people and institutions** exist to run and adapt those assets when shocks arrive.

Three questions guide the work:

1. *Where do we need capacity?*(Which sectors, which locations, which functions.)
2. *What forms should that capacity take?* (Public, private, hybrid; centralised vs. decentralised.)
3. *How do we finance and sustain it over time?* (Investment models, incentives, and governance.)

The answers will vary by country. The underlying logic does not: resilience has to be built, not assumed.

2. Public Investment in Critical Infrastructure

Some capacities are too important, too long-lived, or too low-margin to be left to short-term market signals. In such cases, public investment is a natural starting point.

What Counts as "Critical"

Within RTT, **critical infrastructure** in essential sectors typically includes:

- **Agriculture and food systems:** irrigation networks, grain storage and milling facilities, cold-chain logistics, regional seed banks, testing labs.
- **Energy systems:** transmission and distribution networks, backup generation and storage, regional transformer depots, gas storage and interconnections where relevant.
- **Health and pharmaceuticals:** vaccine production and fill-and-finish sites, basic medical supplies manufacturing, quality-control labs, regional distribution hubs.
- **Water and sanitation:** treatment plants, trunk pipelines, reservoirs and groundwater recharge, flood and drought management systems.
- **Digital infrastructure:** secure data centres for public services, national or regional backbone networks, cyber incident response centres.[1]

Not all of these need to be publicly owned, but many require **public capital** at some stage: to initiate, co-finance, or de-risk investments that private actors would not otherwise make.

Principles for Public Investment

Public investment for resilience should be guided by a few principles:

- **Targeted.** Focus on Tier 1 and key Tier 2 sectors, as identified in the Essentiality Register. Avoid spreading resources thinly across non-essential areas.
- **Additional.** Fill genuine gaps rather than crowding out private capital that would have invested anyway.
- **Durable.** Prioritise assets that provide long-term option value, not just short-term stimulus.
- **Complementary.** Design investments so that they enable private and community actors to plug in, through co-location, shared infrastructure, or service contracts.

Examples include:

- Funding a small number of strategically located multipurpose warehouses that can store food, medical supplies, and emergency equipment.
- Co-financing regional maintenance centres for high-voltage transformers, with clear public-service obligations.
- Establishing a national or bloc-level vaccine platform facility capable of pivoting to new pathogens.

These investments are not glamorous. They often sit outside major cities. But they make the difference between improvisation and continuity when systems are under strain.[2]

3. Incentive Design: Bringing the Private Sector into Resilience

Public investment alone will not be enough. Most essential capacity sits in private hands: farms, mills, logistics companies, manufacturers, software providers, clinics. RTT therefore emphasises **incentive design**: shaping private decisions so that they contribute to resilience rather than undermine it.

Calibrated Incentives

Key tools include:

- **Tax incentives** for investments that reduce chokepoint risks (for example, establishing secondary production lines for critical inputs, or relocating parts of supply chains closer to home markets or allied partners).
- **Subsidised loans or guarantees** for projects that meet resilience criteria but face commercial risk, such as local production of low-margin generic medicines or components.
- **Guaranteed offtake agreements** where governments commit to purchase a portion of output over a period, giving firms confidence to invest in capacity that may be under-used in normal years but vital in crises.[3]

The design challenge is to **reward resilience attributes**, not simply output. That means tying support to:

- Diversification of suppliers and locations.
- Adoption of robust standards (for example, cyber security, redundancy in logistics).
- Demonstrated ability to ramp up production or redirect flows under stress.
- Contribution to domestic and regional labour development.

Procurement as a Lever

Public procurement is a powerful and often underused tool. When governments and public institutions purchase food, energy, medical supplies, or IT services, they can embed **resilience criteria** into tenders and contracts:

- Preference for suppliers that maintain minimum inventory levels domestically.
- Requirements for stress-tested contingency plans.
- Incentives for local or regional co-production in essential sectors.
- Penalties or reallocation clauses when reliability fails without justifiable cause.

By signalling that resilience matters alongside price and quality, governments can create a market for resilience services. Firms that invest in robust systems gain a competitive advantage rather than being undercut by those who free-ride on fragility.

Public–Private Cooperation

Some capacities are best developed jointly. Public–private partnerships (PPPs) can be structured with clear resilience objectives:

- Shared financing of key facilities, ports, storage, data centres, with contractually defined availability and redundancy requirements.
- Joint stockpiling arrangements, where government maintains ownership of reserve stock but uses private facilities and logistics.
- Co-run training centres for essential-sector skills.

These arrangements are not trivial to design. They require competent public partners and transparent oversight. But when done well, they stretch public resources and harness private capacity for public resilience.

4. Strategic Reserves: Stockpiles That Work

Strategic reserves, of food, fuel, medicines, critical components, are among the most visible forms of domestic capacity. They are also among the easiest to mismanage. Reserves that are poorly located, poorly rotated, or poorly governed can create a false sense of security.

RTT treats strategic reserves as **bridges**, not permanent substitutes: they buy time while alternative production or imports are mobilised.

What to Stock

The starting point is the Essentiality Register. For each Tier 1 sector, authorities should identify:

- Which goods are truly critical (for example, grain, select pharmaceuticals, certain fuels, water treatment chemicals, key spare parts).
- Which can be stockpiled safely (physically and financially).
- Which are better addressed through capacity and corridors rather than physical stocks (for example, real-time energy production vs. fuel storage).

Not everything can or should be stored. Focus is essential.

How Much and Where

The concept of **strategic sufficiency** introduced earlier is useful here. For each critical item:

- Estimate **time-to-survive** without new supply (how long society can tolerate shortages before serious harm).

- Estimate **time-to-recover** under plausible disruption scenarios (how long it would take to restore supply through domestic or allied channels).
- Set reserve levels to cover the gap, with a margin for uncertainty.

Location matters as much as volume:

- Reserves should be **geographically distributed** to reduce the risk that a single event (flood, conflict, cyberattack) cuts off access.
- Storage sites should be linked to multiple transport modes (road, rail, water) where possible.
- Responsibility for release should be clearly defined, with protocols for prioritisation.

Examples include:

- Grain reserves near both production regions and population centres.
- Strategic fuel stocks distributed across inland depots, not just coastal facilities.
- Spare transformers and critical components stored in hardened, accessible locations.

Rotation and Governance

Strategic reserves must be **rotated** to avoid spoilage and obsolescence. That requires.

- Integration with regular commercial flows (for example, "first in, first out" systems where reserves are continuously refreshed through normal market activity).

- Contracts with private operators for storage and management.
- Regular audits to verify quantity and quality.[4]

Governance is crucial:

- Clear legal frameworks defining objectives, release conditions, and accountability.
- Separation of technical decisions (when to release) from short-term political pressures where possible.
- Public communication plans to avoid panic or hoarding during release.

Reserves are not a replacement for capacity building. They are one part of a broader architecture that includes domestic and allied production and resilient logistics.

5. Localised Production Nodes and "Anchor" Capacity

Not every essential good needs to be produced domestically in large quantities. But in many cases, it is prudent to maintain **anchor capacity**, a minimum domestic or regional production ability that can be scaled or repurposed during crises.

Why Localised Nodes Matter

Localised production nodes and processing facilities provide:

- **Fallback options** when imported supplies are disrupted.
- **Flexibility** to adapt to local conditions (for example, processing different crop mixes in agriculture, or filling and finishing vaccines using imported bulk).
- **Employment and skills** in regions that host critical infrastructure.
- **Shorter and simpler supply chains** for essential goods, reducing exposure to complex global networks.

This does not mean heavy industry in every region. It means **fit-for-purpose nodes** aligned with each country's strengths and vulnerabilities.

Examples by Sector

- **Agriculture and food:** Regional milling and storage plants, dairies, local seed production, small-scale processing facilities that can operate even when global trade is disrupted.
- **Energy:** Local LPG bottling plants, distributed renewable generation and storage, regional workshops for repair of grid components.
- **Health:** Basic pharmaceutical formulation plants, generic medicine packaging, regional oxygen production, and depots.
- **Water and sanitation:** Localised treatment units, spare parts warehouses, mobile systems for emergency deployment.

East Asian economies provide some examples: Japan, Korea, and Taiwan have preserved certain specialised manufacturing and component capabilities despite global competition, treating them as strategic assets. Nordic countries have maintained local food processing and energy infrastructure even as they trade extensively.

Design and Scaling

Localised nodes do not need to operate at full capacity all the time. Some may function at modest commercial levels during normal periods and be designed to scale in emergencies, supported by:

- Pre-agreed surge contracts.
- Flexible production lines.
- Shared standards and tooling.

The economic question is whether the cost of maintaining such nodes is justified by the option value they provide. In essential sectors, RTT argues that the answer is often "yes."

6. Human Capital and Institutional Depth

Infrastructure and facilities are only as good as the people and institutions that run them. Chapter 6 focused on wages and training. Here, the emphasis is on **institutional depth**: having enough capable organisations, not just individual experts, that can absorb shocks and adapt.

Institutional Redundancy

In many countries, critical functions are concentrated in a few agencies or firms. If a single organisation fails, through cyberattack, mismanagement, or simple overload, the system can struggle to respond.

Institutional depth means:

- Multiple capable organisations in key functions (for example, more than one lab certified to test critical materials; more than one logistics provider able to handle specialised cargo).
- Overlapping expertise across public agencies, so that no single point of institutional failure exists.
- Networks of practice, professional associations, technical forums, that share knowledge and support rapid learning.[5]

Capacity at Different Levels

Resilience requires capacity at:

- **National level:** Strategic planning, major investment decisions, international negotiations, high-level crisis management.

- **Regional level:** Implementation of infrastructure projects, operation of stockpiles, coordination of sector-specific responses.
- **Local level:** Last-mile delivery, community-level adaptation, maintenance, and feedback.

Domestic capacity building should therefore include:

- Strengthening regional and municipal authorities relevant to essentials (for example, water boards, health districts, agricultural extension services).
- Supporting cooperative or community enterprises involved in food systems, energy, or local logistics.
- Ensuring that critical knowledge is not held solely by a few central units.

Institutional depth is less visible than physical projects, but it is just as important. When crises occur, it is often the second-tier institutions, the regional health offices, local grid operators, municipal logistics teams, that make the difference between orderly adaptation and chaos.

7. Education Policy Aligned With Resilience Goals

Education policy is often discussed in terms of competitiveness, innovation, or social mobility. RTT adds another dimension: **resilience alignment**. The question is not only "what skills will the economy need in general?" but "what skills and knowledge will resilience in essential sectors require?"

Three Layers of Alignment

1. **Foundation knowledge for all.**

   All students, regardless of field, should graduate with a basic understanding of how essential systems work: where food comes from, how grids function, what water and sanitation require, how pandemics spread, and what digital systems underpin public services. This creates a baseline of civic literacy that supports informed debate and cooperation in crises.

2. **Targeted pathways for essential sectors.**

   As discussed in Chapter 6, vocational and higher education programmes should be sized and structured to feed essential sectors with sufficient, well-trained personnel. That includes not only technical skills but also systems thinking, risk awareness, and the ability to operate under pressure.

3. **Resilience-oriented research and innovation.**

   Universities and research institutes should be encouraged, through grants, partnerships, and missions, to work on resilience challenges: climate-proofing infrastructure, strengthening supply chain visibility, improving emergency logistics, developing adaptable manufacturing techniques, and designing better governance tools.

Increasingly, governments and regional bodies have experimented with mission-oriented research in areas such as climate transition and health security.[6] RTT suggests integrating **trade and resilience** into this mission logic: inviting academic and industrial collaborations that explicitly tackle vulnerabilities in essential sectors.

Regional and International Dimensions

Education and training for resilience do not need to be purely national. Joint programmes across countries, especially within resilience blocs, can:

- Pool scarce expertise (for example, in advanced agriculture, water management, or cyber defence).
- Foster shared standards and interoperable practices.
- Build professional networks that function as informal crisis channels.

For small or resource-constrained states, regional centres of excellence can offer training that would be difficult to sustain domestically, while still contributing to national capacity when graduates return.

8. Toolkit: A Domestic Capacity Action Plan

To bring the ideas in this chapter together, it is useful to outline a simple action plan.

Toolkit 8 - Domestic Capacity Building Checklist

1. **Identify critical gaps.**

   Using the Essentiality Register and stress-tests, list the top 10 domestic capacity gaps in Tier 1 and 2 sectors (e.g., no domestic vaccine fill-and-finish plant, limited transformer repair capacity, lack of regional grain storage).

2. **Decide the appropriate instrument.**

   For each gap, decide whether public investment, private incentives, procurement reform, or allied cooperation is the primary tool, or a mix.

3. **Design strategic reserves.**

   For a small set of critical goods, define stock levels, locations, rotation mechanisms, and governance rules.

4. **Plan localised nodes.**

   Identify locations where small or medium-sized production or processing nodes can support resilience while also aiding regional economies.

5. **Align training and education.**

   Ensure that programmes exist to supply the skills required by new capacity, technicians, operators, engineers, managers.

6. **Strengthen institutions.**

   Support key agencies, cooperatives, and firms that will run and coordinate essential systems, with attention to both national and local levels.

7. **Set milestones and review.**

   Define what should be in place in 3, 5, and 10 years. Use the RTA's audits to track progress and adjust.

This plan is not exhaustive. But it provides a structured way to move from diagnosis ("we are vulnerable") to construction ("we are less vulnerable than we were").

9. Conclusion: Capacity as a Quiet Form of Power

Domestic capacity building rarely makes headlines. It involves storage sheds rather than summit communiqués, training programmes rather than grand speeches. Yet in a world of increasingly visible shocks and strategic pressure, it is one of the quietest and most important forms of power a state can exercise.

A country that can produce core medicines, maintain its grids, process its food, distribute clean water, secure its networks, and deploy trained people to run these systems is not invulnerable. But it is difficult to coerce and less likely to experience cascading internal crises when disruptions occur. It has room to manoeuvre.

Resilient Trade Theory treats such capacity not as an afterthought, but as a central objective. Building it requires money, time, and political will. It also requires a shift in mindset: away from the assumption that global markets will always deliver, and towards the recognition that **certain capabilities must be cultivated and protected because they are the foundations of collective life**.

The next chapter examines how these domestic capacities interact with **differentiated trade policy**: how to design openness and protection in ways that support, rather than undermine, the effort to build resilience at home.

Endnotes

1. National Academies of Sciences, Engineering, and Medicine. (2022). *Building Resilient Supply Chains: A Strategy for Strengthening U.S. Resilience.*
2. WTO. (2021). *World Trade Report 2021: Economic resilience and trade.* World Trade Organization.
3. Kremer, M., Levin, J., & Snyder, C. (2022). Designing advance market commitments for new vaccines. *Journal of Economic Perspectives, 36*(2), 55–78.
4. OECD. (2021). *Bouncing back: Rebuilding resilient supply chains.* Organisation for Economic Co-operation and Development.

5. Comfort, L. K., Boin, A., & Demchak, C. C. (Eds.). (2010). *Designing Resilience: Preparing for Extreme Events.* University of Pittsburgh Press.
6. Mazzucato, M. (2018). *Mission-Oriented Research & Innovation in the European Union: A Problem-Solving Approach to Fuel Innovation-Led Growth.* European Commission.

CHAPTER 9

DIFFERENTIATED TRADE POLICY

Resilient Trade Theory (RTT) is not an argument against trade. It is an argument against *indiscriminate* trade policy.

For decades, countries were encouraged to liberalise "across the board": cut tariffs, sign as many agreements as possible, and let markets sort out who produced what. The underlying belief was that more openness would almost always mean more prosperity and, by extension, more stability. Recent experience has complicated that story. The same deep integration that brought efficiency has also produced **exposure**, to shocks, to coercion, and to sudden policy shifts in powerful states.[1]

Differentiated trade policy is RTT's response to this reality. It keeps what works, openness, predictability, rule-based exchange, while acknowledging that **not all sectors can be treated alike**. When food, medicine, energy, digital backbones, or key components are at stake, trade rules must reflect their strategic importance. When luxury goods or non-essential services are at stake, openness can remain wide.

This chapter develops that logic. It explores:

- **Friend-shoring and trusted trade corridors**, what they can and cannot do.

- **Tiered trade openness**, aligned with the essentiality tiers developed earlier.
- **Future-ready trade agreements**, including resilience clauses, continuity commitments, and crisis protocols.

The objective is not to provide a blueprint for every country, but to show how RTT translates into concrete trade instruments that **manage risk without sliding into blanket protectionism.**

1. Why Trade Policy Must Be Differentiated

Standard trade advice still emphasises open, stable, and predictable policies as central to growth and resilience. Recent work by the WTO, IMF, and OECD all stress that fragmentation and discretionary restrictions can impose large economic costs, especially for smaller economies.[2] Trade remains a powerful stabiliser: it helps countries smooth local shocks, access essential goods, and tap external demand during downturns.[3]

RTT does not dispute this. Instead, it asks: **under what conditions does openness create unacceptable vulnerability?**The answer depends on three factors:

1. **The sector involved.** A tariff on luxury handbags is not the same as a sudden export ban on staple grains or critical medicines.
2. **The structure of supply.** If imports come from many countries under stable conditions, openness is less risky than when they are concentrated in a few politically contentious sources.
3. **The type of risk.** Physical shocks (pandemics, climate events), cyber risks, and geopolitical leverage play different roles in different sectors.

A differentiated trade policy accepts that **Tier 1 and critical Tier 2 sectors** (as defined in Chapter 4) deserve **different instruments** than Tier 3 and Tier 4 sectors. It does not abandon multilateral rules. It argues that those rules, plus regional and bilateral frameworks, should incorporate a resilience logic rather than assuming stability by default.[4]

In practice, this means three things:

- Being more deliberate about *who* we depend on for essentials.
- Being more careful about *how* commitments are written in trade and investment treaties.
- Being more explicit about *when and how* resilience-related measures may be used.

2. Friend-Shoring and Trusted Trade Corridors

"Friend-shoring" has become one of the defining terms of the current era. It signals a move away from pure cost-based sourcing towards sourcing from **politically trusted partners**, countries seen as stable, rights-respecting, and broadly aligned in their strategic orientation.[5]

The Promise

At its best, friend-shoring can:

- Reduce over-reliance on suppliers in jurisdictions with high coercion risk.
- Encourage investment in **regional production hubs** that are more resilient to shocks.
- Support deeper political and regulatory cooperation among like-minded states.

For example, efforts to diversify semiconductor production beyond a few East Asian locations, or to build critical minerals processing capacity in allied countries, reflect this logic. IMF and OECD analyses suggest that such diversification, when done carefully, can improve resilience without destroying most of the gains from trade.[6]

Trusted trade corridors, specific routes and nodes (ports, rail lines, pipelines, data cables) that are designed, governed, and protected collectively, extend this logic into **infrastructure and logistics.** They embody the idea that resilience is not only about who produces, but also about **how goods move** and **where vulnerabilities lie**.

The Risks

However, friend-shoring and trusted corridors are not a magic shield. They have risks:

- They can **accelerate fragmentation** if used as a blunt instrument to exclude large parts of the world, rather than as a targeted tool for essentials.[7]
- They can be **expensive and inefficient** if they simply duplicate capacity without addressing real bottlenecks.
- They can become a **pretext for hidden protectionism**, with "friend" status used to justify trade diversion unrelated to resilience.

Evidence to date suggests that friend-shoring can improve security in some supply chains, but it is **no guarantee of robustness**: disasters, labor disputes, and cyberattacks can occur in "friendly" jurisdictions as well.[8]

RTT's position is cautious: friend-shoring should be **prioritised for Tier 1 and critical Tier 2 sectors**, and designed with:

- Clear criteria for partner selection (governance quality, rule of law, crisis track record).
- Transparent, jointly developed standards.
- Mechanisms for burden-sharing and mutual support in crises.

For non-essential sectors, broad openness remains preferable, as it supports growth and reduces the risk of large-scale geoeconomic fragmentation.

3. Tiered Trade Openness: Mapping RTT Tiers to Instruments

Differentiated trade policy becomes operational when it is mapped onto **concrete tools**, tariffs, quotas, export controls, investment screening, and regulatory cooperation. RTT proposes a tiered approach aligned with the essentiality structure from Chapter 4.

Tier 1 - Lifeline Sectors

For lifeline sectors, food staples, critical medicines, core energy and grid equipment, drinking water inputs, secure digital backbones, key defence logistics, trade policy should aim for:

- **Secured openness with safeguards**, rather than unconditioned liberalisation.
- **Low or zero tariffs** on essential imports from a diversified set of trusted suppliers.
- **Restrictions or screening** on acquisitions that could place control of critical nodes in hostile hands.
- **Continuity commitments** in trade agreements (see section 4).

In some cases, **temporary protective measures** (tariffs, quotas, local content rules) may be warranted to sustain domestic anchor capacity. But these should:

- Be transparent and justified by clear resilience objectives.
- Have review and sunset provisions.
- Be complemented by allied sourcing arrangements rather than seeking full autarky.

Tier 2 - Enabling Sectors

Enabling sectors, those that support Tier 1 (specialised chemicals, industrial gases, certain metals, logistics hubs, testing services), require:

- **Diverse sourcing** to avoid chokepoints.
- Trade rules that facilitate rapid **re-routing and substitution** when disruptions occur.
- Regulatory cooperation to ensure compatibility of standards.

Tariffs here can also be low, but **concentration risk** should inform trade and investment screening. If global supply is highly concentrated, states may encourage additional capacity in allied regions through incentives and targeted procurement.

Tier 3 and 4 - Important and Discretionary Sectors

For non-essential goods and services, the default remains **high openness**:

- Low or zero tariffs.
- Liberal rules of origin.
- Minimal non-tariff barriers where safety and environment allow.
- Strong multilateral and regional commitments.

These sectors are where traditional comparative advantage and global competition can operate with relatively low systemic risk. WTO and IMF research indicates that maintaining openness here is critical to avoid large welfare losses from fragmentation.[9]

RTT's message is simple: **not all sectors should carry the weight of resilience**. Concentrate resilience-motivated restrictions on the essentials, and keep the rest of the economy as open and dynamic as possible.

4. Designing Future-Ready Trade Agreements

Traditional trade agreements focus on tariffs, quotas, services access, and investment protections. Future-ready agreements, consistent with RTT, add a new layer: **resilience architecture**.

Resilience Clauses

Resilience clauses explicitly recognise that parties may need to take measures to protect essential sectors in crises, while also seeking to **prevent abuse** of such measures. Elements might include:

- A **shared definition** of essential sectors and critical goods, based on mutual lists that can evolve over time.
- Agreement that, in defined emergency conditions, parties may temporarily prioritise domestic supply or redirect exports, but with notification obligations and time limits.
- Mutual commitments to avoid export bans on certain goods (for example, vaccines, staple grains) except under clearly defined circumstances and with minimal disruption to partners.[10]

These clauses are not easy to negotiate. But they offer something better than today's mix of **ad hoc restrictions and legal grey zones**, which can undermine trust during crises.

Continuity Commitments in Essentials

Beyond flexibility, future-ready agreements can include **continuity commitments**:

- Parties may agree to supply each other with minimum volumes of particular goods, even during stress, subject to shared scarcity rules.
- They may establish **priority lanes** in ports, customs, and logistics for shipments under these commitments.
- They may develop **joint stockpiles** governed by common rules, especially for small states that cannot afford large reserves alone.

The health sector offers a precedent. Some regional frameworks already include provisions for mutual assistance during pandemics and coordinated procurement of medical countermeasures.[11] RTT suggests extending this logic to a broader set of essential sectors.

Crisis Coordination Protocols

Trade agreements can also embed **crisis coordination mechanisms**:

- Dedicated committees or task forces that convene when pre-defined triggers occur (for example, export restrictions on listed goods, major corridor disruptions).
- Shared data platforms for tracking stock levels, bottlenecks, and alternative routes.
- Joint communication strategies to reduce panic and speculation.

These mechanisms help turn **resilience blocs** from rhetorical clubs into operational communities.

Guarding Against Protectionism

Critics worry that resilience language in trade agreements could become a **backdoor for protectionism**. That risk is real. It can be mitigated by:

- Clearly limiting resilience-motivated measures to **pre-defined essential sectors**.
- Requiring measures to be **least trade-restrictive** consistent with the objective.
- Subjecting measures to **review panels** or independent advice within agreed timelines.
- Embedding **sunset clauses** and renewal conditions.

WTO's 2021 World Trade Report notes that resilience and openness can be mutually supportive when rules are transparent and cooperative, rather than unilateral and opaque.[12] RTT's approach builds on that insight.

5. Balancing Resilience and Fragmentation Risks

Differentiated trade policy walks a narrow path. Too little attention to resilience leaves countries exposed; too much fragmentation undermines growth and global problem-solving.

IMF simulations suggest that severe geoeconomic fragmentation, driven by broad-based trade and technology restrictions, could reduce long-run global output by up to 7 per cent, with disproportionate effects on emerging and low-income economies.[13] OECD and WTO analyses also stress that **over-correction**, reshoring everything, rigid friend-only supply chains, can backfire, increasing costs without significantly improving resilience.[14]

RTT addresses this tension in three ways:

1. **Scope control.**

   Restrictive or reshoring measures are limited to clearly defined Tier 1 and critical Tier 2 sectors. Everywhere else, the presumption of openness stands.

2. **Design discipline.**

   Measures are assessed not only for their political appeal, but for their *actual contribution* to resilience: do they reduce chokepoint risk, improve time-to-recover, or diversify sources in meaningful ways?

3. **Cooperative orientation.**

   Whenever possible, resilience is pursued through **cooperative arrangements**, resilience blocs, shared corridors, joint stockpiles, rather than unilateral restrictions.

In other words, RTT is not about "less trade" but about **smarter, more intentional trade** in a subset of strategically important domains. That distinction is central when speaking to partners, investors, and multilateral institutions.

6. Regional Illustrations

The logic of differentiated trade policy will express itself differently across regions. A few brief illustrations help show how RTT might map onto real contexts.

Europe: Open Strategic Autonomy in Practice

The European Union has embraced "open strategic autonomy" as a guiding idea, maintaining openness while reducing critical dependencies in areas like health, energy, and digital.[15] In trade policy, this has led to:

- More attention to **vulnerability mapping** and monitoring of critical supply chains.
- Proposals to build **resilience partnerships** with trusted suppliers of critical raw materials, semiconductors, and health products.
- Discussions about export controls and investment screening in security-sensitive technologies.

RTT would encourage the EU to:

- Further formalise **essential sector lists** and resilience clauses in its trade agreements.
- Distinguish more explicitly between Tier 1/2 and Tier 3/4 sectors, keeping the latter as open as possible.
- Use its size to anchor **resilience corridors** that benefit neighbouring regions as well.

East Asia and the United States: Technology and security

East Asia and the United States are at the centre of technology-intensive trade, semiconductors, digital services, advanced manufacturing. The region has already seen:

- Export controls and counter-measures in chips and critical inputs.
- Moves to diversify production away from single locations.
- Early discussions of **technology alliances** and shared standards.

RTT would suggest:

- Concentrating restrictive measures on genuinely strategic nodes (for example, specific chip generations, key equipment) rather than broad-brushing entire sectors.
- Building **multi-country production clusters** (for example, Japan-Korea-US, or Taiwan-US-EU partnerships) with continuity commitments.
- Ensuring that essential civilian uses, health, energy, basic communications, are shielded as much as possible from the fallout of broader strategic competition.

Americas and the Global South: Food, Minerals, and Unequal Impact

Latin America, parts of Africa, and other resource-rich regions supply food, energy, and minerals to much of the world. Geoeconomic fragmentation and uncoordinated friend-shoring could, in principle, **bypass** some of these suppliers, reducing their export earnings and development prospects.[16]

At the same time, these regions are vulnerable to **import disruptions** in fertilisers, medical products, and technology. RTT would argue for:

- Regional **resilience pacts** that secure intra-regional trade in essentials (for example, grains, fertilisers, basic medicines) with shared stockpiles.
- Carefully designed friend-shoring arrangements that ensure **value-added production** and skills stay in the region, rather than repeating extractive patterns.
- Active participation in WTO and other forums to shape resilience rules in ways that protect development space.

These examples are sketches, not blueprints. Their purpose is to show that differentiated trade policy must be **context-specific**, even while drawing on common principles.

7. Toolkit: Building a Differentiated Trade Strategy

For policymakers wanting to bring RTT's principles into their trade portfolio, a structured approach helps.

Toolkit 9 - Steps for Differentiated Trade Policy

1. **Map sectors to tiers.**

   Use the Essentiality Register to categorise sectors into Tiers 1–4. Confirm which sectors, if any, are misaligned with current trade policy (for example, fully liberalised but heavily concentrated essentials).

2. **Diagnose dependencies.**

   For Tier 1 and critical Tier 2 sectors, identify key imports and exports, supplier concentration, and exposure to jurisdictions with high coercion or climate risk.

3. **Set resilience objectives.**

   Define what "strategic sufficiency" means in each essential sector: minimum domestic capacity, maximum acceptable concentration, desired allied coverage.

4. **Align trade instruments.**

   Adjust tariffs, quotas, procurement rules, and investment screening to support these objectives, **but only in essentials**. Avoid using resilience to justify across-the-board protection.

5. **Develop friend-shoring and corridor plans.**

   Identify trusted partners and corridors for essential goods. Negotiate frameworks that include continuity commitments, crisis protocols, and shared standards.

6. **Update trade agreements.**

   Where feasible, renegotiate or add protocols that include resilience clauses, essential-goods lists, and mechanisms for emergency coordination.

7. **Monitor fragmentation impact.**

   Track the economic and diplomatic consequences of resilience measures. If evidence shows that costs are high and resilience gains small, be prepared to adjust.

8. **Communicate clearly.**

   Explain to domestic and international audiences that differentiated policy aims to *protect essentials while keeping the rest open*, not to close borders or dismantle multilateralism.

Used consistently, this toolkit can help governments avoid two common errors: **over-securitising trade**, or pushing resilience concerns aside until the next crisis.

8. Conclusion: Trade Policy as Design, Not Drift

For many years, trade policy operated on autopilot: more agreements, lower tariffs, broader coverage. That era is over. Shocks, coercive practices, and strategic rivalries have made it clear that **who we trade with, in what, and on what terms** matters far more than we assumed.

Resilient Trade Theory does not call for abandoning openness. It calls for transforming trade policy from drift to **design**:

- Design that recognises a hierarchy of sectors, lifeline, enabling, important, discretionary.
- Design that uses friend-shoring and trusted corridors to reinforce, not replace, multilateral rules.

- Design that embeds resilience clauses, continuity commitments, and crisis protocols in trade agreements.
- Design that deliberately limits fragmentation by confining restrictive measures to where they are genuinely needed.

If this is done well, countries and blocs can remain deeply engaged in the global economy while reducing their exposure to catastrophic disruption and coercion. If it is not done at all, or if it is done badly, the likely outcome is a mix of unmanaged vulnerability and costly, politically driven fragmentation.

The next chapters zoom back out, examining how differentiated trade policy interacts with **social cohesion, diplomacy, and global justice**. Trade is one piece of the resilience puzzle, but it is a piece that shapes almost all the others.

Endnotes

1. WTO. (2021). *World Trade Report 2021: Economic resilience and trade.* World Trade Organization. wto.org+1
2. IMF. (2023). *Geo-Economic Fragmentation and the Future of Multilateralism.* International Monetary Fund; IMF. (2023, August 28). *The High Cost of Global Economic Fragmentation.* IMF+2elibrary.imf.org+2
3. WTO. (2021). *World Trade Report 2021: Economic resilience and trade* (Chapter C: The role of trade in economic resilience). wto.org
4. IISD. (2021). Increased trade cooperation would build economic resilience at the WTO. International Institute for Sustainable Development. iisd.org
5. Maihold, G. (2022). *A New Geopolitics of Supply Chains: The Rise of Friend-Shoring.* Stiftung Wissenschaft und Politik. Stiftung Wissenschaft und Politik (SWP)

6. European Central Bank. (2023). *Friend-shoring global value chains: a model-based assessment*; OECD. (2025). *Supply Chain Resilience Review: Navigating Risks.* European Central Bank+1
7. Mikic, M. (2023). *Supply Chain Resilience, Friend-shoring, and the Pursuit of Security.* T20 Policy Brief. t20ind.org
8. OECD. (2025). *Supply Chain Resilience Review: Navigating Risks* (discussion of geographic de-risking limits). OECD
9. IMF. (2023). *Review of the Role of Trade in the Work of the Fund*; WTO. (2021). *World Trade Report 2021.* IMF+1
10. UNESCAP. (2020). *Lessons from regional trade agreements to boost trade resilience.* unescap.org
11. WHO. (2022). *Strengthening pandemic preparedness: Simulation exercises and stress tests*; see also regional joint procurement mechanisms in the EU and African Union. Single Resolution Board
12. WTO. (2021). *World Trade Report 2021: Economic resilience and trade* (overview). wtocenter.vn
13. IMF. (2023). *Geo-Economic Fragmentation and the Future of Multilateralism.* IMF+1
14. OECD. (2025). *Supply Chain Resilience Review: Navigating Risks*; WTO. (2021). *World Trade Report 2021.* OECD+1
15. Schmitz, L. (2023). Understanding the rise of open strategic autonomy in EU trade policy. *Journal of Common Market Studies*; JRC. (2023). *Assessing Open Strategic Autonomy.* globalpolicyjournal.com+3onlinelibrary.wiley.com+3iri.jrc.ec.europa.eu+3
16. IMF. (2023, October 3). *Geoeconomic Fragmentation Threatens Food Security and Clean Energy Transition.*

CHAPTER 10

SOCIAL COHESION AS ECONOMIC INFRASTRUCTURE

Resilient Trade Theory (RTT) has, up to this point, spoken largely in the language of sectors, systems, and institutions. We have talked about grids and ports, seed systems and stockpiles, trade corridors and stress-tests. All of that is necessary. None of it is sufficient.

Because when things go wrong, systems depend on people, not only as workers and managers, but as neighbours, citizens, and communities. The willingness to follow emergency guidance, to accept rationing, to keep working in essential roles, to adapt without violence, these are not automatic behaviours. They are products of **social cohesion**: trust, shared identity, a sense that burdens and benefits are distributed fairly.

This chapter makes a simple, but often neglected claim: **social cohesion is economic infrastructure.** It is as important to resilience as substations and warehouses. You cannot legislate it into being at the moment of crisis; you have to build it in advance.

We will look at three core themes:

- how economic resilience and national unity reinforce (or undermine) each other.
- how cooperative ownership, small and medium enterprises (SMEs), and community wealth strategies can root resilience in everyday life.
- how inclusive planning can turn potentially divisive decisions into sources of stabilisation rather than conflict.

The aim is to bring RTT down to the level where people actually live and decide.

1. Economic Resilience and National Unity

It is tempting to treat "social cohesion" as a soft variable, important in theory, but hard to integrate into economic design. In reality, it is a hard constraint. When social cohesion is weak, even well-designed systems struggle under stress. When social cohesion is strong, imperfect systems can be patched, improvised, and carried through.

We can think of cohesion as a kind of **latent capacity**: an invisible reserve of trust and willingness to cooperate that can be drawn upon when formal mechanisms are strained. Research on disasters and crises shows this repeatedly. Communities with higher levels of trust, associational life, and perceived fairness tend to experience lower mortality, faster recovery, and fewer episodes of unrest, even when material conditions are similar.[1]

In an RTT framework, social cohesion matters in at least four ways.

1.1 Compliance without Coercion

During crises, states often need to ask a great deal of their citizens: stay at home, change work patterns, accept temporary shortages, follow rationing rules, make space for emergency uses of infrastructure. If people widely believe that government is incompetent or corrupt, or that rules are being applied unfairly, compliance drops and coercion becomes the default tool.

Coercion is expensive, politically, financially, and socially. It also wears out quickly. A state that enters a crisis with high trust and a reputation for fairness can instead rely more on **voluntary compliance and self-organisation**, freeing its limited enforcement capacity for truly critical tasks.

1.2 Burden-Sharing and Perceived Fairness

Resilience strategies almost always involve trade-offs. Some regions host infrastructure with environmental or social impacts. Some sectors receive targeted support while others face more competition. Some groups are asked to work through crises while others can shelter.

Whether these trade-offs are accepted depends less on formal rules than on **perceptions of fairness**. If people in one region feel that they always bear costs while others reap benefits, restraint can erode. If essential workers feel invisible or disposable, their willingness to keep systems running cannot be assumed.

RTT therefore treats **equity as a stabiliser**: the more people feel that "we are in this together, and the rules are not rigged," the easier it becomes to manage shocks without fracture.[2]

1.3 Protection Against Polarisation

Economic dislocation, regional decline, and perceived abandonment are fertile ground for polarisation. When parts of a country feel permanently excluded from growth and decision-making, they become more susceptible to narratives that frame national institutions as illegitimate or hostile. That, in turn, undermines the coordination needed for resilience.

Resilience-oriented policy, if badly designed, can make this worse, for example, if "strategic sectors" are all located in capital regions, or if resilience investments bypass communities that have already experienced decades of neglect. Conversely, if resilience is used to **reconnect marginalised regions to national purpose**, it can dampen polarisation instead of feeding it.

1.4 Legitimacy of Hard Choices

Finally, social cohesion provides **legitimacy** when leaders make hard choices. In a prolonged crisis, some decisions will be contested no matter what, which industries to bail out, which corridors to prioritise, which imports to favour. Without a baseline of trust and participation, those decisions are read as arbitrary or corrupt. With it, even unpopular measures can be accepted as necessary and temporary.

In short, social cohesion is not a feel-good accessory to strong systems. It is one of the main reasons those systems hold.

2. How Efficiency-First Policies Undermined Cohesion

If we want to use RTT to rebuild cohesion, we have to be honest about how earlier models contributed to its erosion.

The efficiency-first version of globalisation tended to generate **sharp winners and losers**:

- Some regions became hubs for finance, technology, or services; others saw their manufacturing or agricultural bases hollowed out.
- Some firms and workers were able to plug into global value chains; others were displaced or pushed into precarious roles.
- Some groups benefited from cheaper imports; others bore the cost of sudden competition without meaningful adjustment support.[3]

Three patterns matter particularly for cohesion.

2.1 Regional Dislocation

Regions whose traditional industries faced intense import competition often saw **job loss, declining tax bases, and outmigration of the young.** In some countries, this produced what has been called a geography of "left-behind places": areas with weaker public services, higher social stress, and growing resentment at central government.[4]

In a resilience context, these are often the very regions that host critical infrastructure, ports, energy facilities, logistics nodes, food systems. Losing their confidence and cooperation is not just a moral problem; it is a strategic vulnerability.

2.2 Precarious Work in Essential Sectors

As supply chains were optimised for cost, many essential functions were shifted to **subcontracted, temporary, or informal labour**. Cleaning staff in hospitals, warehouse workers in logistics hubs, seasonal agricultural labourers, and many care workers found themselves in roles that were indispensable but insecure.

When crises hit, these are the people we suddenly label "essential", and then expect them to work in unsafe or exhausting conditions without a corresponding claim to security or voice. That is not a stable equilibrium.

2.3 Hollowed-Out Local Institutions

Local financial institutions, cooperatives, and mutuals have withered in many places, replaced by distant decision-making and short-term capital. Where local anchor institutions survive, a university, a large hospital, a locally-rooted firm, they can still act as stabilisers. But in many communities, the sense that "decisions are made elsewhere" is pervasive.

RTT does not romanticise the past or ignore the gains from trade and integration. It simply notes that **a system which repeatedly and predictably leaves certain groups and places behind is not resilient**. Social cohesion must therefore be treated as a design objective, not an accidental by-product.

3. Cooperative Ownership and Community Anchors

One practical way to root resilience in social cohesion is through **ownership and control structures** that give communities a stake in essential systems.

Cooperatives, mutuals, and community-owned enterprises are not a cure-all. Some fail; some become inward-looking; some are captured by local elites. But when well-designed, they provide three assets that are directly relevant to RTT:

- **Embeddedness.** They tend to be anchored in place, rather than footloose.
- **Voice.** Users and workers have channels to influence decisions.
- **Trust.** People are more likely to cooperate with institutions they part-own and understand.

3.1 Food Systems

In agriculture and food, cooperatives have long provided mechanisms for small producers to:

- pool resources and gain access to storage, processing, and markets
- negotiate better terms with buyers
- invest collectively in resilience measures (for example, irrigation or soil conservation)

From East Asian rice cooperatives to European dairy co-ops and Latin American producer associations, these structures can support both **economic viability** and **community stability**.[5]

Under RTT, policy can:

- support cooperatives in strategic regions with technical assistance and access to finance
- include them in resilience planning for food security
- use public procurement to anchor demand for cooperative-produced staples

3.2 Energy and Infrastructure

Community and municipal energy projects, local grids, district heating, renewable generation owned in part by residents, can:

- reduce dependence on distant providers
- keep a share of economic value in the community
- encourage local participation in energy-saving and emergency plans

Nordic countries, parts of Germany, and some US municipalities provide examples of this model.[6] In a resilience context, community energy projects can be paired with

microgrids and storage that keep critical local services running when national grids are under stress.

3.3 Finance and Mutual Support

Credit unions, mutual savings banks, and community development finance institutions (CDFIs) can:

- provide patient capital for SMEs in essential sectors
- help stabilise local economies during difficult times
- operate with governance structures that reflect member priorities

Policies that favour only large, centralised financial institutions can inadvertently weaken these local stabilisers. RTT suggests that **financial diversity**, including mission-driven local institutions, is part of resilience, not merely an historical curiosity.[7]

4. SMEs and Community Wealth as Resilience Engines

Large firms will remain central to many essential sectors. But **small and medium enterprises (SMEs)** and anchor institutions can play a disproportionate role in linking resilience to social cohesion.

4.1 SMEs in Essential Sectors

SMEs often:

- occupy niche positions in supply chains (specialised components, maintenance services, local logistics)
- provide employment in smaller cities and rural areas
- have strong relationships with local communities

Their weakness is vulnerability to shocks: limited capital buffers, dependence on a few clients, and exposure to sudden demand swings. When they fail, resilience suffers, fewer repair options, thinner local capacity, and more concentrated supply chains.

Resilience-oriented policy can:

- prioritise SME access to resilience-related procurement (for example, maintenance contracts, local storage management)
- offer targeted credit lines or guarantees for SMEs that invest in resilience-relevant capabilities
- support SME networks and clusters in essential sectors (for example, regional maintenance and repair ecosystems for critical infrastructure)

4.2 Community Wealth Building

"Community wealth building" is a term used to describe strategies that use **local assets and procurement** to keep more economic value circulating in a region.[8] For RTT, this approach is directly relevant:

- Public institutions (hospitals, schools, local authorities) can use their procurement to support **locally-rooted firms and cooperatives** in food, maintenance, and services.
- Infrastructure projects can be designed to maximise local employment and ownership, where feasible.
- Land and real estate used for resilience projects (for example, storage facilities, training centres) can be structured to benefit local communities through ground rents or shared governance.

The point is not to close local economies off from trade, but to ensure that **resilience investments do not simply extract**

value. When communities see tangible benefits, jobs, contracts, facilities — they are more likely to support needed projects.

4.3 Anchor Institutions

Hospitals, universities, large public agencies, and some private firms function as **anchor institutions**, organisations that are unlikely to move and that have a significant footprint in local economies.

Resilience strategies can work with anchors to:

- coordinate emergency responses at local level
- co-design training programmes for essential skills
- align procurement with SME and cooperative development
- host public forums and planning processes

In Pacific Island states, for example, public utilities and regional universities have played anchor roles in climate adaptation and disaster preparedness, linking technical work with community engagement. Similar patterns appear in parts of Europe and North America.[9]

5. Inclusive Planning as a Tool of Stabilisation

Resilience planning involves choices that affect land use, employment patterns, infrastructure siting, and risk distribution. If those choices are made behind closed doors, they risk igniting conflict. If they are made through **inclusive, transparent processes**, they can do the opposite: build legitimacy, uncover local knowledge, and reduce resistance.

Inclusive planning does not mean that every decision becomes a referendum. It means that:

- affected communities are consulted early rather than presented with faits accomplis

- trade-offs are explained in clear language, not hidden in jargon
- there are visible channels for dissent and modification

Three tools are particularly relevant.

5.1 Participatory Scenario Exercises

Table-top exercises and scenario workshops are not only for officials. They can be adapted for public use:

- inviting community representatives, SMEs, cooperatives, and local authorities to explore "what if" scenarios, severe weather, supply chain disruption, cyber incidents
- mapping how different groups would be affected
- jointly identifying practical mitigation measures

This kind of exercise has two effects: it **improves plans** by incorporating local knowledge, and it **builds a shared understanding** of why certain measures (for example, stockpiles, corridor investments, emergency protocols) are needed.

5.2 Deliberative Forums

Citizens' assemblies, deliberative polls, and other structured forums can be used to address specific resilience questions:

- Where should a new storage facility be sited, and under what conditions?
- How should rationing or priority access be managed in a prolonged disruption?
- What principles should guide the use of export controls or emergency powers?

Evidence from democratic experiments suggests that when people have time, information, and the chance to deliberate with others, their judgments become more nuanced and their willingness to accept trade-offs increases.[10]

For RTT, deliberative processes are a way to **embed ethics and social acceptability** into resilience decisions.

5.3 Transparency in Metrics and Audits

Chapter 7 emphasised the role of resilience audits. Their findings should not be confined to technical circles. Publishing accessible summaries:

- helps citizens understand where vulnerabilities lie
- demonstrates that government takes resilience seriously
- creates pressure to follow through on recommendations

Making metrics visible, for example, days of strategic stock, concentration levels, vacancy rates in essential occupations, can also support public debate. It invites scrutiny, but it also builds trust when progress is real.

6. Regional Vignettes: Cohesion and Resilience in Practice

While RTT is a forward-looking framework, there are real-world examples that illustrate aspects of the link between cohesion and resilience.

6.1 Japan: Social Discipline and Local Organisation

Japan's experience with earthquakes, tsunamis, and industrial accidents has shown the importance of **neighbourhood-level organization**, volunteer fire brigades, community councils, and local disaster plans. These sit atop a culture where, despite tensions, there is a strong expectation of collective responsibility.

In economic terms, local cooperatives, SMEs, and municipal utilities have played stabilising roles in recovery. While far from perfect, this combination of social discipline and local institutional depth offers a glimpse of how **social fabric and infrastructure interact.**[11]

6.2 Nordic Europe: Welfare, Trust, and Continuity

Nordic countries are often cited for their high levels of social trust and strong welfare systems. From a resilience perspective, these features matter because:

- people trust that basic needs will be met
- essential workers are relatively well-supported
- regional disparities, while present, are less stark than in many other systems

This does not immunise them against shocks, as energy and migration crises have shown, but it gives them **room to adjust** without immediate fracture.

6.3 Pacific Islands: Community Networks and Climate Stress

Small island states in the Pacific face acute climate threats and limited material resources. Yet social and cultural cohesion, extended family networks, and customary land tenure systems have often provided **informal safety nets** that cushion shocks.

At the same time, outmigration and economic pressures are testing these systems. Here, RTT would highlight the need to **reinforce traditional forms of cohesion with formal resilience investments**, rather than treating them as substitutes for state responsibility.[12]

6.4 North America and Europe: The Cost of Fracture

By contrast, some advanced economies have discovered that high GDP and strong formal institutions do not guarantee smooth crisis management. Polarisation, regional alienation, mistrust of elites, and online disinformation have all made it harder to achieve coherent responses to pandemics, energy shocks, and economic dislocation.

From an RTT perspective, these cases are warnings: **if cohesion is neglected, even wealthy states with sophisticated infrastructure can find themselves unable to execute resilience plans.**

7. Toolkit: Making Social Cohesion Part of Resilience Policy

To keep social cohesion from remaining an abstract aspiration, resilience strategies should include concrete steps.

Toolkit 10 - Social Cohesion and Resilience Checks

1. **Map social fault lines.**

   Identify regions, sectors, and groups that have experienced repeated losses or neglect in previous economic transitions. Treat these as priority areas for inclusive resilience planning.

2. **Anchor resilience investments locally.**

   Where possible, tie new infrastructure, stockpiles, and nodes to local employment, cooperative ownership, or SME contracts, especially in left-behind regions.

3. **Support essential-sector workers visibly.**

   Implement minimum liveable wages and improved conditions in essential sectors and communicate clearly why these measures are being taken.

4. **Strengthen local institutions.**

   Invest in municipal capacity, community enterprises, and local finance institutions that can act as partners in resilience.

5. **Institutionalise participation.**

   Build deliberative and consultative mechanisms into major resilience decisions, siting, rationing rules, emergency protocols, rather than improvising consultation ad hoc.

6. **Monitor trust and legitimacy.**

   Use surveys, focus groups, and qualitative methods to track public trust in institutions and perceptions of fairness around resilience measures.

7. **Align communication with reality.**

   Avoid over-promising. Explain constraints and trade-offs honestly. Trust is easier to lose than to rebuild.

8. **Treat cohesion as an investment area.**

   Recognise that programmes which reduce extreme regional and social disparities, in health, education, and economic opportunity, are also investments in resilience.

These steps do not replace hardware or trade rules. They make those investments usable when they matter most.

8. Conclusion: The Social Foundations of Resilient Trade

Resilient Trade Theory began with critical goods: food, energy, medicine, digital infrastructure. It moved through strategic capacity, labour systems, governance, and differentiated trade policy. This chapter has argued that beneath all of these lies something quieter, but more fundamental: **the quality of relationships within a society**.

A country or bloc can have carefully calibrated trade rules, well-funded stockpiles, and technically sophisticated plans. If large parts of its population feel abandoned, exploited, or systematically unheard, that structure will shake under pressure. Conversely, a society that has invested in cohesion, fair treatment of essential workers, shared benefits from resilience investments, functioning local institutions, inclusive planning, will be able to improvise and adapt even when plans are incomplete.

Social cohesion, then, is not "soft" relative to the "hard" infrastructure of resilience. It is the substrate on which everything else rests.

RTT invites policymakers to treat cohesion as they would any other critical asset: to measure it, protect it, and build it deliberately. The following chapters extend this logic outward, exploring how diplomacy and global alliances can support not just national resilience, but a wider architecture of **shared stability and justice** in a world that will remain turbulent.

Endnotes

1. Aldrich, D. P. (2012). *Building resilience: Social capital in post-disaster recovery*. University of Chicago Press.
2. Norris, F. H., Stevens, S. P., Pfefferbaum, B., Wyche, K. F., & Pfefferbaum, R. L. (2008). Community resilience as a metaphor, theory, set of capacities, and strategy for disaster readiness. *American Journal of Community Psychology, 41*(1–2), 127–150.
3. Autor, D., Dorn, D., & Hanson, G. (2016). The China shock: Learning from labor market adjustment to large changes in trade. *Annual Review of Economics, 8*, 205–240.

4. Rodríguez-Pose, A. (2018). The revenge of the places that don't matter (and what to do about it). *Cambridge Journal of Regions, Economy and Society, 11*(1), 189–209.
5. Birchall, J. (2013). *Resilient communities: Co-operatives in times of crisis.* International Labour Organization.
6. Bauwens, T., Gotchev, B., & Holstenkamp, L. (2016). What drives the development of community energy in Europe? The case of wind power cooperatives. *Energy Research & Social Science, 13*, 136–147.
7. Mertens, D., Thiemann, M., & Volberding, P. (Eds.). (2021). *The reinvention of development banking in the European Union.* Oxford University Press.
8. Kelly, M. (2019). *The making of a democratic economy: Building prosperity for the many, not just the few.* Berrett-Koehler.
9. Pelling, M., & Uitto, J. I. (2001). Small island developing states: Natural disaster vulnerability and global change. *Environmental Hazards, 3*(2), 49–62.
10. Fishkin, J. S. (2018). *Democracy when the people are thinking: Revitalizing our politics through public deliberation.* Oxford University Press.
11. Yamori, K. (2012). Disaster preparedness and community governance: The case of Japan. *International Journal of Disaster Risk Reduction, 1*, 34–40.
12. Weir, T., Dovey, L., Orcherton, D., & Holland, E. (2017). Social and cultural issues raised by climate change in Pacific Island countries: An overview. *Asia Pacific Viewpoint, 58*(2), 169–182.

CHAPTER 11

DIPLOMACY AND GLOBAL RESILIENCE ALLIANCES

Up to this point, Resilient Trade Theory (RTT) has spoken mostly in national or bloc-level terms: how a country classifies sectors, builds capacity, treats essential workers, designs its trade policy. But no matter how disciplined a country becomes at home, it will still face threats that do not respect borders, pandemics, climate shocks, cyberattacks, and cascading supply chain disruptions.

Resilience, in other words, cannot be purely national. It has an **outward face**. That outward face is diplomacy.

This chapter explores how RTT extends into foreign policy. It asks a set of simple but demanding questions:

- How can countries move from defensive, zero-sum resilience toward **mutual reinforcement**?
- What would a **resilience bloc** or alliance actually look like in practice?
- How can new arrangements avoid recreating familiar North–South divides?
- And how do we protect against the risk that "resilience diplomacy" simply becomes a new label for fragmentation and power politics?

We will look at four main elements:

1. A shift in trade diplomacy from price to principle.
2. The design of resilience blocs and trusted corridors.
3. Multilateral preparedness pacts for shared threats.
4. A justice lens on access to strategic resources.

The goal is not to propose a single grand architecture, but to show how RTT can inform a **more cooperative resilience order** rather than a world of isolated fortresses.

1. From National Resilience to Shared Security

The instinct to look inward after a shock is understandable. When supply chains fail and shelves empty, it is tempting to think: "If only we did everything ourselves." Yet the evidence is stubborn: turning inward, especially in small and medium economies, **does not reliably produce resilience**. It often raises costs, reduces diversity of supply, and leaves countries more exposed to their own local shocks.

Trade and interdependence, handled with care, remain powerful resilience assets. When a crop fails at home, imports can prevent hunger. When a storm damages domestic infrastructure, access to external equipment and expertise speeds recovery. When demand plunges in one region, exports to others keep firms afloat. The World Trade Organization's work on resilience makes this point clearly: open, rules-based trade has cushioned many shocks, even as it has transmitted others.

RTT therefore does not call for a world of sealed-off economies. It calls for **intentional interdependence**: a pattern of relationships in which countries:

- know which partners they rely on for essentials

- have some say in how those relationships are governed
- share information, stockpiles, and contingency plans
- accept that, in crises, obligations run in both directions

That is where diplomacy comes in. Resilience alliances are not an optional extra for foreign policy, they are an organising principle.

2. Redefining Trade Diplomacy: From Price to Principle

Traditional trade diplomacy has been dominated by a few recurring themes: market access, tariff levels, investment protections, occasionally labour or environmental standards. The underlying metric of success has often been **price and volume**: more trade at lower cost.

RTT suggests an additional lens: **principle**. This does not mean moralising every negotiation. It means recognising that, for certain sectors and flows, questions like "*Can we rely on you when things go wrong?*" and "*Will your decisions suddenly weaponise our dependencies?*" are just as important as tariff lines.

A resilience-oriented diplomacy therefore:

- treats some sectors, health, food, core energy, key digital infrastructure, as **security-relevant** in their own right, not just economic
- asks for **continuity commitments** in these sectors: advance rules on export restrictions, priority access, and crisis coordination
- pays attention to **governance quality** in partner countries: rule of law, transparency, and crisis performance

- anchors trade in **shared norms** where possible: equity in health emergencies, climate responsibility, respect for basic rights

Recent negotiations around the WHO Pandemic Agreement illustrate this shift. The emerging accord links health security to obligations on data sharing, technology transfer, local production, and the avoidance of unnecessary disruptions to trade in health products during emergencies.

This is exactly the kind of evolution RTT anticipates: trade rules that explicitly acknowledge resilience goals, rather than treating shocks as externalities to be dealt with later.

3. Building Resilience Blocs

One of RTT's more ambitious ideas is the formation of **resilience blocs**: clusters of countries that commit to mutual support in essential sectors and shared preparedness.

This does not need to resemble a defensive alliance. Think of it more as a **public goods club**: members agree to contribute to and benefit from common capacities they could not efficiently secure alone.

3.1 What Defines a Resilience Bloc?

A genuine resilience bloc would have three core features:

1. **Shared mapping of essentials.**

   Members agree on a list of critical goods and services, vaccines, certain medicines, key grains, grid components, data routing, strategic minerals, and keep that list updated.

2. **Mutual continuity commitments.**

   Members pledge, as far as possible, not to cut each other off from these essentials in crises; and to coordinate any necessary restrictions to minimise harm inside the bloc.

3. **Joint investments and corridors.**

   Members co-invest in production, stockpiles, and logistics: shared storage facilities, multi-country manufacturing hubs, protected shipping routes, interoperable digital infrastructure.

Some early steps in this direction already exist. The Supply Chain Resilience Initiative between Australia, India, and Japan, for example, explicitly aims to diversify and strengthen regional supply chains through cooperation rather than autarky. The OECD also documents growing experiments in shared risk monitoring and best-practice exchange on supply chain resilience among like-minded economies.

These initiatives are narrow and sector-specific. RTT invites countries to think more broadly and systematically.

3.2 Design Principles

A resilience bloc designed along RTT lines would pay attention to:

- **Diversity within the bloc.** Members should not all share the same vulnerabilities; otherwise shocks may still hit everyone at once.
- **Inclusion of smaller economies.** Small states often host strategically located ports, cables, or resources. Their needs and voices must be integrated, not tacked on.
- **Conditional openness.** Blocs should aim to complement, not replace, multilateral rules—remaining open to others where risk allows, and avoiding "closed club" dynamics in non-essential sectors.

The aim is not to build new empires under a resilience label. It is to build **mutual insurance networks** that reduce the temptation for every country to scramble on its own in the next crisis.

4. Multilateral Preparedness Pacts

Alongside regional blocs, there is a need for **global preparedness pacts** that address threats no region can handle alone. The clearest example today is the WHO Pandemic Agreement—recently finalised after years of negotiation.

4.1 Lessons from the Pandemic Treaty

The pandemic accord's draft and final texts contain several elements that resonate strongly with RTT:

- A commitment to **strengthen local and regional production** of health countermeasures, particularly in low- and middle-income countries.
- Provisions for **pathogen access and benefit-sharing**, linking access to surveillance data with fair access to resulting vaccines and treatments.
- Language encouraging parties to **avoid measures that unnecessarily disrupt supply chains**, even while they take steps to protect their populations.

In other words, the treaty attempts to reconcile national preparedness with the reality that health security is deeply global, both biologically and economically.

RTT would regard this as a prototype: a sector-specific global resilience pact linking **capacity building, equity, and trade disciplines** in one framework.

4.2 Beyond Pandemics: Climate and Cyber

Other domains are moving in similar directions, though more slowly:

- **Climate adaptation and loss-and-damage mechanisms** seek to support vulnerable states with finance, technology, and early-warning systems, recognising that climate shocks will otherwise generate spiralling humanitarian and geopolitical crises.
- **Cybersecurity frameworks**, often still informal, attempt to set expectations for behaviour around critical infrastructure and cross-border attacks, sometimes including commitments to assistance and information sharing after incidents.

RTT's contribution here is conceptual: it offers a language in which to treat these agreements not as isolated technical instruments, but as part of a **broader global resilience architecture**, one that acknowledges interdependence without demanding naïve trust.

5. Global Justice and Shared Access to Strategic Resources

If resilience alliances and pacts become the preserve of wealthy or strategically powerful states, they risk reinforcing the very instabilities they claim to address. In a world where vaccine access, critical mineral processing, and even basic food security remain unequally distributed, **justice is not an optional extra**; it is a stability condition.

5.1 The Equity Problem

The COVID-19 experience made this painfully clear. While some countries secured early and abundant access to vaccines and diagnostics, others waited months or years for meaningful coverage. This was not only morally troubling; it also undermined global control of the pandemic and fuelled mistrust of international institutions.

Current pandemic agreement texts respond by embedding principles of **equity, solidarity, and technology transfer**, and by encouraging financing and capacity-building for production in developing countries.

Similarly, debates around supply chain "de-risking" and friend-shoring have raised concerns that rich countries will lock in preferred access to critical minerals, chips, or green technologies, while poorer states are left with volatile commodity markets and little value-added. The IMF and OECD repeatedly warn that geoeconomic fragmentation will hit emerging economies hardest, particularly those reliant on trade and external finance.

5.2 Justice as Stabiliser

RTT therefore argues that **global justice is a structural part of resilience**, not a charitable add-on:

- If low-income food-importing countries cannot secure grain in crises, global instability rises, through migration, conflict, and political contagion.
- If African, Asian, or Latin American producers of critical resources are systematically excluded from higher-value segments of resilient supply chains, resentment and strategic realignment will follow.
- If small island states are left to manage climate-driven displacement and infrastructure damage alone, their statehood itself comes under strain.

Resilience alliances that ignore these dynamics will be brittle. Those that **share access and build capacity beyond their core members** will be more durable.

5.3 What Shared Access can Look Like

Practically, this might mean:

- Binding commitments to allocate a portion of vaccine or medicine stocks to a global pool in pandemics, managed with transparent criteria.
- Co-financing of manufacturing and processing facilities for critical goods in developing regions, with fair intellectual property arrangements.
- Open, rules-based access to resilience-critical transport corridors (ports, canals, air routes), with agreed mechanisms for prioritising humanitarian and essential cargo.
- Multilateral facilities that help poorer countries afford resilience measures, stockpiles, early-warning systems, redundant infrastructure, without sacrificing other development goals.

None of this is straightforward. But the underlying logic is simple: **a resilience order that works only for the already secure will not hold.**

6. Risks: New Fragmentation, Old Power Asymmetries

Any move to build resilience alliances carries two major risks.

6.1 Fragmentation

First, resilience language can be used to justify **broad decoupling and bloc-building** that extend far beyond essentials. Aggressive reshoring and across-the-board friend-only sourcing would, according to OECD and IMF modelling, impose large long-run GDP and welfare losses—particularly on smaller economies and the Global South.

RTT's tiered approach is designed to hold the line: focus restrictive or alliance-based measures on **clearly defined lifeline sectors**, and keep non-essentials as open as possible. Resilience blocs must be explicit that they are not general-purpose economic clubs; otherwise they risk fuelling exactly the fragmentation their members claim to oppose.

6.2 Asymmetry and Dominance

Second, alliances can reproduce **old hierarchies**. Larger states may use resilience as a lens to lock in preferential access to resources, dictate standards, or offload adjustment costs onto smaller partners. "Partnership" language can mask highly unequal bargaining power.

RTT therefore advocates for:

- governance arrangements in alliances that guarantee smaller states meaningful voice
- transparency in how benefits and burdens are shared
- mechanisms for dispute resolution that are not controlled by a single power centre

Without some version of this, "resilience alliances" risk becoming a new vocabulary for strategic competition rather than a genuine attempt at shared security.

7. Toolkit: Designing a Resilience Alliance Strategy

For governments thinking about how to align their diplomacy with RTT, a practical checklist can help.

Toolkit 11 - Steps for Resilience-Oriented Diplomacy

1. **Clarify your essentials map.**

   Enter alliances knowing which sectors and goods you consider lifeline or critical. Do not outsource this definition.

2. **Assess current dependencies.**

   For each essential, identify your main foreign suppliers, choke points, and political risk profile. This will tell you where alliances matter most.

3. **Segment your partnerships.**

   Distinguish between:

   – strategic partners for essentials

   – broad trade partners for non-essentials

   – adversarial or high-risk counterparts where dependence should be reduced

4. **Identify potential resilience bloc partners.**

   Look for countries that combine: governance compatibility, complementary capacities, geographic logic, and a track record of cooperation.

5. **Co-design commitments.**

   Work with partners to define essential lists, continuity commitments, crisis protocols, and joint investments. Aim for precision, not rhetorical generalities.

6. **Integrate justice from the start.**

   Ask who is missing: small states, regional neighbours, resource suppliers. Design finance, technology transfer, and access arrangements that give them a stake.

7. **Embed resilience in trade and sectoral agreements.**

   Add resilience clauses, preparedness provisions, and collaboration mechanisms in health, climate, and cyber frameworks, not just tariffs and quotas.

8. **Monitor fragmentation risk.**

   Track how resilience-motivated measures affect your openness, your partners' opportunities, and global institutions. Adjust if the costs begin to outweigh the security gains.

9. **Invest in diplomatic capacity.**

   Train trade and foreign service officials in resilience thinking: systems, risk, and the interdependence of health, climate, digital, and economic security.

This is not a one-off process. As threats evolve, alliances must be reviewed and sometimes re-drawn. The point is to move from **reactive crisis diplomacy** to a more deliberate, resilience-aware foreign policy.

8. Conclusion: Toward a Cooperative Resilience Order

Resilient Trade Theory began with a domestic question: what must a country be able to secure for itself, and what can it safely trade? That question does not disappear at the border. It simply changes shape.

We now live in a world where no state, no matter how large, can fully insulate itself from transnational shocks. Pandemic pathogens, extreme weather, cross-border cyber incidents, and systemic supply disruptions will all be part of the strategic landscape for the foreseeable future. In that world, **resilience without cooperation is an illusion**.

The task, then, is not to choose between openness and security. It is to **re-design openness** on terms that acknowledge real risks and shared obligations. That means:

- trade diplomacy that includes resilience and equity alongside prices and quotas
- resilience blocs that pool capacity without hardening into closed camps
- global preparedness pacts that connect local production and fair access with disciplines on disruptive measures
- and a justice lens that recognises that resilience built for a few will not protect many

If we succeed, the result will not be a perfect or orderly system. It will be a landscape of overlapping alliances, imperfect treaties, and evolving norms, a **cooperative resilience order** in which shocks still occur, but fewer of them cascade into catastrophe.

If we fail, the likely future is a patchwork of competing fortresses, each trying to hoard security at others' expense. That path leads not to safety, but to deeper instability and loss.

RTT offers a different path: one in which **national strength and shared security are seen not as opposites, but as mutually reinforcing goals**. The diplomatic work to build that path will be difficult and slow. But in a century defined by common risks, it is hard to imagine a more necessary project.

Endnotes

1. World Trade Organization. (2021). *World Trade Report 2021: Economic resilience and trade.* WTO.
2. OECD. (2025). *OECD Supply Chain Resilience Review: Navigating risks.* OECD.
3. WHO. (2025). *WHO Pandemic Agreement* (Resolution WHA78.1). World Health Assembly; WHO. (2025, April 16). *Member States conclude negotiations and make significant progress on draft pandemic agreement* (news release).
4. International Institute for Sustainable Development. (2021). Increased trade cooperation would build economic resilience at the WTO. IISD.
5. OECD. (2024). *Promoting resilience and preparedness in supply chains.* OECD Trade Policy Paper.
6. IMF. (2023). *Estimating the costs of geoeconomic fragmentation.* International Monetary Fund.
7. National Board of Trade Sweden. (2020). *Improving economic resilience through trade – should we rely on our own supply?* Swedish Ministry for Foreign Affairs.
8. WHO. (2025). *WHO Pandemic Agreement: Text agreed by 21 February 2025* (draft).
9. The Global Observatory. (2025, May 20). How the landmark pandemic agreement addresses technology transfer and access to pandemic response products.
10. OECD. (2021). *Resilience of global supply chains.* European Parliament Research Service briefing drawing on OECD work.

PART IV

Critiques, Extensions, and Global Applications

CHAPTER 12

COMMON CRITIQUES AND MISCONCEPTIONS

Any serious framework must be able to withstand criticism. If Resilient Trade Theory (RTT) is going to be useful to economists, policy professionals, and political leaders, it cannot live in an echo chamber of agreement. It has to sit in the same room as its critics and answer.

This chapter does three things.

First, it looks at the most common *political* critique: that RTT is simply protectionism in new clothes. Second, it addresses the *strategic* critique: that RTT is a step toward isolationism and bloc politics. Third, it engages with *orthodox* economic objections, especially those rooted in comparative advantage, dynamic efficiency, and political economy.

The goal is not to claim that RTT is flawless. It is to clarify what RTT is, and what it is not, so that debate can take place on solid ground rather than on caricature.

1. Why Critiques Matter for Resilient Trade Theory

RTT is a normative framework: it suggests how countries *should* think about trade, security, and social stability. That alone is enough to attract scepticism. But there is a deeper reason criticism matters.

Resilience is easily misused. The language of "national security" and "strategic sectors" has always carried the risk of being turned into a catch-all justification for almost anything: subsidies, favours, trade barriers, or centralisation of power. If RTT is not clear about its boundaries, it risks becoming a convenient label for old ideas.

So criticism is a kind of stress-test. If RTT cannot respond in a disciplined way to the charge of protectionism, or if it cannot answer mainstream economic concerns without collapsing into slogans, it will not be worth much in practice.

With that in mind, we can start with the one accusation RTT will hear most often.

2. "Isn't This Just Protectionism?"

On the surface, it is an understandable question. RTT advocates:

- support for domestic and allied capacity in essential sectors
- selective trade restrictions or safeguards where critical vulnerabilities exist
- public investment and procurement criteria that prioritise resilience

To someone steeped in decades of liberalisation, that can look suspiciously like an invitation to roll back openness.

2.1 What Protectionism Actually Looks Like

Classical protectionism is not hard to recognise. It usually:

- applies broad-based trade barriers across many sectors
- is justified in vague terms ("saving jobs," "supporting national champions")

- has weak review mechanisms
- often persists long after any initial rationale has disappeared

It treats imports themselves as a problem, and it tends to favour certain domestic producers simply because they are domestic, not because they are strategically important.

2.2 How RTT is Different

RTT is more constrained, and more demanding.

1. **Narrow scope.**

   RTT focuses its most intrusive tools on clearly defined *Tier 1* and critical *Tier 2* sectors, those truly essential for survival and continuity. It does not call for protective measures in the wide range of sectors that are economically important but not strategically critical.

2. **Transparent criteria.**

   It asks that sectors be classified through an explicit process, with published criteria and periodic review. The idea is that "strategic" status should be earned, not claimed. This is a very different posture from blanket pleas for protection.

3. **Time-bound and reviewable.**

   Where tariffs, quotas, or local content rules are used, RTT expects them to be revisited: are they still needed? Have they actually reduced vulnerability? Protection without review becomes rent-seeking; RTT proposes guardrails to prevent that.

4. **Open by default in non-essentials.**

   In everything that is not essential, luxury goods, most consumer services, cultural products, discretionary sectors, RTT is supportive of openness. Trade, competition, and foreign investment in these areas are not treated as threats; they are treated as engines of growth and innovation.

5. **Resilience, not domestic favours, as the test.**

   The question RTT asks of any measure is: *does it actually reduce systemic vulnerability or coercion risk in a measurable way?*If the answer is no, then the measure is not consistent with RTT even if it benefits domestic actors.

Put simply: where protectionism is usually *producer-driven* ("help us compete"), RTT is *system-driven* ("reduce risk in essentials"). The overlap exists, but it is not complete.

2.3 When the Critique is Valid

There is, however, a valid warning embedded in the protectionism critique. Any framework that legitimises selective restrictions can be misused.

RTT therefore accepts that in some contexts, the right answer to the question "Is this just protectionism?" will be "Yes, it has become that", and that the remedy is to reapply the internal tests:

- Is the sector genuinely essential?
- Are the measures the least trade-distorting tools available?
- Are there allied or multilateral options that would achieve the same effect more efficiently?
- Is there a sunset or review mechanism?

If those questions cannot be answered convincingly, RTT would regard the measure as a departure from its intent, not a faithful application.

3. "Doesn't This Lead to Isolationism and Blocs?"

A second line of criticism looks less at tariffs and more at geopolitics. Friend-shoring, resilience blocs, continuity clauses, it all sounds, to some ears, like the early stages of a fragmented world: competing camps, divided markets, and a collapse of multilateralism.

RTT takes that risk seriously. But the picture is more nuanced.

3.1 The Myth of Inevitable Isolation

RTT's core claim is not that countries should do everything at home. It is that they should:

- retain or build *strategic sufficiency* in a limited set of essential sectors
- cultivate deep, reliable relationships with **trusted partners** for essentials they do not, or cannot, produce
- keep the rest of their economies as open as possible

In this picture, isolationism is not a goal. The goal is to shape interdependence so that no single external actor can credibly threaten a country's basic functioning.

For many small and medium economies, genuine autarky is implausible. They lack the resources, market size, or technological base to supply all essentials internally at reasonable cost. For them, **trusted interdependence** is not a retreat from openness; it is a way to avoid being trapped by it.

3.2 Blocs vs. Alliances

The word "bloc" carries historical weight: rigid alliances, zero-sum thinking, and the risk that non-members become marginalised. RTT uses the idea more narrowly.

A *resilience bloc* is not an exclusive trade club. It is a group of countries that:

- share critical infrastructure and production capacity in defined sector
- commit to continuity of supply in emergencies
- coordinate investments and stockpiles to avoid duplicated vulnerabilities

Outside those sectors, bloc members can and should trade widely. The purpose is not to close off, but to make sure that **when shocks occur**, they do not immediately turn inward and hoard at each other's expense.

The risk, of course, is that blocs drift from this narrow resilience purpose towards broader economic closure. That risk is real. RTT's answer is to insist on *scope control* and *clear design*:

- define essential sectors explicitly
- limit alliance commitments to those sectors
- keep non-essential sectors governed by multilateral and open regional rules

If this discipline is lost, the critique that RTT promotes fragmentation becomes stronger. If it is maintained, RTT can coexist with, and even support, multilateral systems by reducing panic responses during crises.

4. Orthodox Economic Critiques

Beyond political and strategic concerns, RTT also attracts critiques from more orthodox economic perspectives. These usually fall into three families:

1. **Comparative advantage and welfare losses**;
2. **Dynamic efficiency and innovation**;
3. **Political economy and rent-seeking**.

Each has force. Each also rests on certain assumptions that RTT makes explicit and, in some cases, rejects.

4.1 Comparative Advantage and the Cost of Deviation

The most straightforward critique is this: if RTT encourages countries to produce some goods at home that they could import more cheaply, it is asking them to **sacrifice gains from trade**. If many countries follow this path, global efficiency and incomes will be lower than they would otherwise be.

This critique is correct in a narrow sense. RTT openly accepts that in some essential sectors, countries may pay more per unit in normal times than they would under pure cost minimisation.

The disagreement is about what is being optimised:

- Traditional models optimise *average outcomes* under an assumption of reasonably stable conditions and low probability of extreme, systemic shocks.
- RTT optimises *system survival and autonomy* under an assumption that extreme shocks, disruptions, and coercive practices are no longer rare.

Once that assumption changes, the relevant question is not "Is this the cheapest supplier today?" but "What is the expected cost of relying on this structure over the next decade, including the cost of disruption and coercion?"

In that sense, RTT is not anti-comparative advantage. It is an attempt to **expand the definition** to include reliability, risk concentration, and option value. The resulting pattern may still favour specialisation and trade in many areas, but not at the expense of basic security.

4.2 Innovation and Dynamic Efficiency

Another orthodox concern is that protective measures, even targeted ones, may reduce the pressure to innovate. Firms that enjoy sheltered domestic markets are less likely to upgrade technology, improve quality, or adopt new processes. Over time, this can leave essential sectors technologically backward, with all the knock-on effects that implies.

RTT takes this concern seriously. It suggests three design responses:

1. **Open competition inside the "safe" zone.**

   Essential sectors can be protected in terms of *location and control* (for example, domestic or allied ownership and capacity) without being insulated from **domestic and allied competition**. Multiple firms can compete to provide resilient services under common rules.

2. **Benchmarking and performance standards.**

   Public investment and procurement in essential sectors can be tied to performance metrics: efficiency, quality, environmental standards, and innovation targets. Support is conditional, not automatic.

3. **Use of global knowledge.**

   Even when production is local or regional, technology can still be global. Licensing, joint ventures, and collaborative research can bring frontier techniques into essential sectors without requiring full openness to foreign control.

In other words, RTT argues that **resilience and innovation are not inherently opposed**. They can be designed to reinforce each other if protection is targeted, contestable, and periodically reviewed.

4.3 Political Economy and Capture

Perhaps the most serious orthodox critique is not economic in the narrow sense, but political. It goes like this:

Once you create a category of "strategic" sectors and allow them special treatment, those sectors, and others, will lobby to be included. Over time, the list will expand, the measures will become permanent, and the system will look a lot like old industrial policy: captured, inefficient, and biased.

History offers plenty of examples where appeals to "national security" or "strategic importance" were used to shield uncompetitive industries, reward political allies, or pursue opaque agendas. This is not a theoretical risk; it is an empirical one.

RTT's response is partly technical and partly ethical:

- **Technical guardrails**, transparent criteria, independent review, sunset clauses, and public audits—can reduce the ease with which interests hijack the framework. They cannot eliminate capture, but they raise the cost of abuse and make it more visible.
- **Ethical framing**, presenting RTT explicitly as a *duty to protect populations* rather than a license to distribute favours, matters too. It changes the questions citizens and journalists ask. It creates a standard against which actions can be judged.

In the end, RTT does not claim to solve political economy. It claims that **doing nothing**, leaving resilience to "the market" while shocks and coercion proliferate, also has political economy costs: bailouts, ad hoc interventions, and opaque crisis decisions when things fail. The choice is not between a politically neutral status quo and a politicised RTT; it is between different ways of managing an already politicised reality.

5. When RTT Should Say "No"

An honest framework must also be able to say "no" to proposals presented in its name. RTT is no exception.

There are at least four types of measures that **should not be endorsed** under RTT, even if they are framed in the language of resilience:

1. **Blanket tariffs or export bans** on broad categories of goods without clear evidence that they relate to essential sectors or genuine chokepoints.
2. **Permanent subsidies or protections** for sectors that are no longer essential, or where vulnerability has been addressed through other means.
3. **Measures that clearly violate basic equity**, for example, hoarding life-saving medical supplies in ways that dramatically worsen outcomes in poorer countries without making the initiator meaningfully safer.
4. **Policies that significantly erode openness in non-essential sectors**, with little or no demonstrated benefit for essential-sector resilience.

In those cases, RTT is not a shield. It is grounds for critique: the framework has been invoked, but its internal tests have not been met.

There will also be edge cases, areas where reasonable people can disagree. Is a particular technology genuinely essential? Does a given measure produce enough reduction in vulnerability to justify the cost? Here, RTT cannot provide automatic answers, but it can at least frame the debate around *risk, evidence, and trade-offs*, rather than slogans.

6. RTT as Complement, Not Replacement

Finally, some orthodox critics worry that RTT is trying to **replace** the mainstream economic approach to trade, rather than complement it. They hear calls for resilience and fear that the accumulated knowledge of decades, on trade patterns, welfare effects, development strategies, will be swept aside.

That is not the intention.

RTT is built on the recognition that:

- globalisation has delivered real gains, including in many developing countries
- trade and specialisation remain crucial for growth and poverty reduction
- but the world we inhabit now has **different risk properties** than the one in which much of the post-war trade architecture was developed

Those different risk properties, systemic shocks, deliberate economic coercion, climate-induced disruptions, require an additional layer of thinking. RTT is that layer. It asks:

- Where do traditional assumptions about stability no longer hold?
- Where do we need redundancy, local capacity, or allied commitments to complement pure efficiency?

- How can we adjust trade rules and domestic policies without undoing the benefits of openness?

In that sense, RTT is not an alternative to mainstream trade theory; it is an attempt to **update its domain of application.** The hope is not that economists and policymakers abandon their existing tools, but that they use them in concert with a more explicit view of risk, power, and human vulnerability.

7. Conclusion: Learning From Critique

Critiques of RTT fall into three main categories:

- political (protectionism, isolationism)
- economic (efficiency, innovation)
- institutional (capture and misuse)

Some are overstatements. Some identify real dangers. All are useful.

They remind us that RTT must remain:

- **narrow and disciplined** in its use of intrusive tools
- **honest about costs** in terms of efficiency and growth
- **transparent and reviewable** to minimise capture
- **openly engaged** with mainstream economic analysis, not allergic to it

If RTT is applied carelessly, it will confirm its critics' worst suspicions. If it is applied with rigour, it can help countries and blocs navigate a world where shocks are more frequent, interdependence is more politicised, and the stakes of failure are higher.

The next chapters turn to concrete applications and to the larger context: how RTT can be adapted across regions, and how it might evolve as climate, technology, and demographics reshape the global environment. But those applications will only be meaningful if the framework they rest on is capable of standing in the face of critique, not as a final answer, but as a serious participant in the argument.

Endnotes

1. Rodrik, D. (2011). *The Globalization Paradox: Democracy and the Future of the World Economy*. W. W. Norton.
2. Baldwin, R. (2016). *The Great Convergence: Information Technology and the New Globalization*. Harvard University Press.
3. World Trade Organization. (2021). *World Trade Report 2021: Economic resilience and trade*. WTO.
4. International Monetary Fund. (2023). *Geo-Economic Fragmentation and the Future of Multilateralism*. IMF.
5. Krugman, P. (1993). What do undergrads need to know about trade? *American Economic Review, 83*(2), 23–26.
6. Hausmann, R., Rodrik, D., & Velasco, A. (2008). Growth diagnostics. In *The Washington Consensus Reconsidered: Towards a New Global Governance* (pp. 324–355). Oxford University Press.
7. Aiginger, K., & Rodrik, D. (2020). Rebirth of industrial policy and an agenda for the twenty-first century. *Journal of Industry, Competition and Trade, 20*(2), 189–207.
8. Evenett, S. J. (2019). Protectionism, state discrimination, and international business since the onset of the Global Financial Crisis. *Journal of International Business Policy, 2*(1), 9–36.

CHAPTER 13

REGIONAL APPLICATION MODELS

Resilient Trade Theory (RTT) is, at its core, a set of principles: classify what is essential, build strategic capacity, protect lifeline sectors without collapsing openness, and anchor all of it in social cohesion and ethics. But theories only become meaningful when they touch places with actual names.

This chapter looks at **regional and national application models**, not as perfect embodiments of RTT, but as living labs that show how fragments of the framework already exist in practice.

We will focus on:

- the **European Union** as a bloc-level experiment in "open strategic autonomy"
- five national examples : **Taiwan, Finland, the United Arab Emirates (UAE), Vietnam, and Brazil**, each illustrating different aspects of Resilient Trade Theory
- and finally, quieter forms of "silent resilience" in the broader Global South

The aim is not to declare winners, but to see what can be learned, what to emulate, what to avoid, and how these patterns might inform future RTT applications.

1. Why Regional Application Matters

RTT is not designed as a one-size-fits-all template. A small island state, a continental union, and an export-led Asian economy will not, and should not, pursue resilience in the same way.

Yet there are recurring questions that all of them must answer:

- Which sectors are **non-negotiable**?
- Where do we insist on **domestic or allied capacity**, and where can we stay fully global?
- How much redundancy is enough, and who pays for it?
- How do we maintain openness in non-essentials while de-risking essentials?

Regional and national cases show how these questions look when they collide with history, geography, politics, and path dependency. They also reveal something important: **many countries have been doing pieces of RTT for years**, often without naming it as such.

What RTT offers is a way to gather those fragments into a coherent picture, and to make the trade-offs explicit instead of implicit.

2. The European Union: Open Strategic Autonomy in Practice

The European Union (EU) is perhaps the closest thing we have to a **bloc-level RTT laboratory**. After the euro crisis, the migration crisis, COVID-19, and the energy shock triggered by Russia's invasion of Ukraine, the EU has been forced to rethink how it balances openness and security.

2.1 From Single Market to "Open Strategic Autonomy"

Over the past five years, "open strategic autonomy" has become a central phrase in EU policy, particularly in trade, industrial, and foreign economic policy. The European Commission and multiple EU bodies describe it as the Union's ability to "make its own choices and shape the world around it" while remaining committed to open, fair trade and diversified global value chains.

In RTT terms, this is very close to the idea of **intentional interdependence**:

- Open where it is safe
- Protective where it is necessary
- Constantly alert to over-reliance on hostile or unstable suppliers

The EU has translated this into:

- **vulnerability mapping** of critical raw materials, health products, and digital infrastructure
- new **industrial policy instruments** (for example, the Chips Act, the Critical Raw Materials Act) to build anchor capacity in semiconductors and key inputs
- more assertive use of **trade defence** and **investment screening** where security risks are identified

2.2 Strengths and Tensions

From an RTT perspective, three strengths stand out:

1. The EU treats resilience as a **bloc-wide project**. Smaller member states gain access to a scale of investment and bargaining power they could not achieve alone.

2. It has begun to **classify sectors** explicitly (critical raw materials, key technologies, health products), rather than relying on generic lists of "priorities".
3. It is trying, at least in principle, to hold onto **openness in non-critical sectors**, recognising that broad reshoring is neither efficient nor necessary for resilience.

At the same time, there are tensions:

- Some fear "open strategic autonomy" may slip into ordinary protectionism by another name, especially if crisis rhetoric is used to justify broad industrial support with weak targeting.
- There are **internal asymmetries**: larger member states can move faster on public investment and industrial policy, while smaller ones risk being treated mainly as markets or buffer zones.
- The EU still relies heavily on external partners for many essentials, from fertilisers to pharmaceuticals ingredients, and is in the early stages of fully aligning its trade agreements with its resilience ambitions.

For RTT, the EU is a reminder that **resilient trade at bloc level is a continual negotiation**, not a settled state. But as a direction of travel, it is the clearest large-scale move toward an RTT-compatible model we currently have.

3. Taiwan: Strategic Capacity and the "Silicon Shield"

If Europe is the laboratory for bloc-level autonomy, **Taiwan** is the starkest example of resilience built around a single, extraordinary strategic sector: semiconductors.

3.1 Concentrated Excellence, Concentrated Risk

Taiwan's semiconductor ecosystem, anchored by TSMC and surrounded by a dense network of suppliers, designers, and service firms, has become central to global production of advanced chips. This has brought GDP growth, high-quality jobs, and significant bargaining power: Taiwan's so-called "silicon shield" is based on the assumption that its centrality to the global economy discourages conflict.

From an RTT angle, Taiwan represents:

- **hyper-specialisation** in a Tier 1 enabling sector (chips underpin almost every modern essential system);
- **deep domestic capacity**: world-leading R&D, manufacturing, and industrial organisation;
- **embedded interdependence**: its chips are everywhere, and its inputs come from everywhere.

Yet this success is also a vulnerability. Concentrating so much of the world's advanced chip production on a single, geopolitically exposed island creates a structural fragility for everyone.

3.2 Adaptive Industrial Policy

Recent policy moves in Taipei show an attempt to manage this risk without abandoning the model:

- The government's "trusted industry" and industrial upgrading plans explicitly seek to **enhance resilience** in core sectors such as semiconductors, defence-related technologies, and cybersecurity, while encouraging diversification into other advanced fields.

- Taiwan has pursued **friend-shoring-like partnerships** with the United States, Japan, and Europe, co-investing in facilities abroad while keeping critical capabilities at home.
- It has also signalled that reshoring "half" of its U.S.-bound chip production to American soil, as recently floated by U.S. officials, is a step too far, a reminder that **resilience and leverage are a two-way street.**

For RTT, Taiwan illustrates both the power and the limits of strategic capacity:

- Its semiconductor complex is an almost textbook example of **strategic sufficiency at world-class level**, but
- its overall resilience still depends on external partners for energy, food, and imported inputs, and
- the balance between **sharing capacity and preserving leverage** is constant and delicate

4. Finland: Institutionalised Preparedness

If Taiwan shows what strategic industrial capacity looks like, **Finland** shows what it means to build resilience into **institutions, law, and everyday expectations.**

4.1 Security of Supply as a National Doctrine

Finland's history, wars, isolation risks, a harsh climate, long borders, has produced a culture that treats preparedness not as an eccentric hobby, but as a mainstream responsibility. The **National Emergency Supply Agency (NESA)** is the core institution coordinating this effort.

NESA and its wider network:

- manage **strategic stocks** of food, fuel, and critical medical and industrial supplies
- organise **security of supply "pools"** that bring together public agencies and firms across sectors like energy, logistics, food, and health
- develop strategies and exercises to maintain functionality in severe crises

Households, too, are integrated into this mindset. Public campaigns encourage every family to maintain a **72-hour emergency kit** and basic self-sufficiency at home. Recent coverage has highlighted that Finland can draw on national grain reserves lasting many months, and produces a large share of its own food even in a challenging climate.

4.2 Lessons for RTT

Finland is not perfect, it remains import-dependent in many sectors and fully integrated into European trade structures, but it offers at least three lessons that resonate strongly with RTT:

1. **Preparedness is normalised.** It is built into law, budget, education, and culture, not left to ad hoc crisis responses.
2. **Public-private cooperation is formalised.** Firms and agencies co-plan, exercise, and share responsibility. This is precisely the sort of institutional depth RTT emphasises.
3. **Households are treated as partners, not spectators.** The social dimension of resilience is recognised and actively cultivated.

In RTT language, Finland is an example of how **domestic capacity, governance, and social cohesion** can reinforce each other in a high-trust democracy.

5. United Arab Emirates: Food Security and Directed Resilience

The **United Arab Emirates (UAE)** offers a different angle: resilience pursued through **targeted, top-down strategies** in a resource-rich, import-dependent state.

5.1 Food Security as Strategic Priority

Recognising its extreme dependence on food imports and exposure to climate stress, the UAE adopted a **National Food Security Strategy 2051**, with the stated goal of becoming a global leader on innovation-driven food security and ranking at the top of global indices.

Key elements include:

- increasing domestic production of certain foods through heavy investment in **agritech and controlled-environment agriculture** (vertical farms, hydroponics)
- diversifying import sources and investing in food production abroad
- building **strategic reserves** and improving logistics
- establishing a dedicated governance structure for food security.

Recent analyses note the ambition to raise local production to around half of national needs by 2051, backed by generous public and sovereign wealth funding.

5.2 Strengths and Trade-offs

From an RTT perspective, the UAE shows:

- a clear recognition that **food is Tier 1**, and cannot be left purely to spot markets
- a willingness to use **state capital and planning** to accelerate capacity in essential sectors
- a strong focus on **technology and global partnerships** to bridge resource constraints

At the same time, there are trade-offs:

- heavy technological solutions can be energy-intensive and vulnerable to disruptions in input supply
- land and water use abroad can raise questions of **land grabs** and local justice in host countries
- highly centralised models risk shallow social embedding if community and labour dimensions are not addressed

The UAE, in short, illustrates a bold, state-driven version of RTT in essentials, with open questions about long-term sustainability and equity.

6. Vietnam: Trade Integration and Adaptive Resilience

Vietnam is one of the most trade-dependent economies in Asia, with total trade reaching well over its GDP and a steady climb up global value chains.

6.1 Deep Openness with Resilience Concerns

Vietnam's development path has been built on **export-oriented industrialisation**, foreign direct investment, and integration into regional and global supply chains, electronics, textiles, footwear, and more recently higher-value manufacturing.

This openness has delivered growth and poverty reduction. But it has also left Vietnam:

- exposed to shifts in global demand and trade tensions
- reliant on imported inputs and technologies
- vulnerable to climate impacts in key regions (for example, the Mekong Delta)

Recent policy debates and reports, including a World Bank "Viet Nam 2045" assessment, stress the need to **upgrade participation in global value chains** while managing new risks, from automation to geopolitics.

6.2 Emerging RTT-like Elements

Signs of RTT-aligned thinking include:

- efforts to **diversify markets and partners**, reducing over-reliance on a small number of destinations
- growing emphasis on **institutional capacity** as a "fourth pillar" of sustainable value chains, alongside economic, social, and environmental dimensions
- investments in **infrastructure and logistics** to reduce vulnerability to chokepoints

Vietnam is not yet running a resilience-first trade strategy; its priority remains growth and upgrading. But it is increasingly aware that **resilience and competitiveness must be pursued together**, not in sequence. For RTT, Vietnam is a reminder that in many emerging economies, the challenge is not over-protection but how to **build resilience without interrupting the development path** that trade made possible.

7. Brazil: Energy, Food, and Strategic Redundancy

Brazil brings another dimension: a large, resource-rich democracy that has used energy and agricultural policy to build a degree of **strategic redundancy**, particularly in fuels and food.

7.1 Biofuels and Energy Security

For decades, Brazil has invested in **biofuels**, ethanol from sugarcane and, increasingly, corn; biodiesel from soy and other feedstocks, as a way to reduce dependence on imported oil and to leverage its agricultural base. Recent moves to raise mandatory blending levels in gasoline and diesel are expected to make Brazil effectively **self-sufficient in gasoline**, cutting import needs and strengthening its energy security.

At the same time, Brazil's role in the G20's Global Biofuel Alliance and its new industrial policies explicitly link **energy security, industrial upgrading, and climate objectives**.

7.2 Food Production and Export Power

Brazil is also a major exporter of soy, beef, poultry, and other staples, making it a key player in global food security, and a country with significant leverage over downstream markets. This brings both opportunities and ethical responsibilities: decisions taken in Brasília on land use, export policy, and environmental enforcement can reverberate in food prices and climate systems worldwide.

7.3 Nexus Challenges

From an RTT lens, Brazil illustrates the **nexus problem**: energy, agriculture, water, and climate are tightly interlinked. Policies that improve resilience in one domain can undermine it in another if poorly designed.

- Expanding biofuels can enhance fuel security, but risks crowding out food crops or driving deforestation if governance is weak.
- Agricultural export strength provides foreign exchange and bargaining power, but can leave domestic systems vulnerable if internal distribution and social equity are not addressed.

Brazil's experience suggests that **resilience in resource-rich countries is as much about governance and environmental stewardship as it is about capacity per se**.

8. "Silent Resilience" in the Global South

Beyond headline strategies and well-branded policies, there is a quieter category of resilience practice in many Global South countries, what we might call **silent resilience**.

These are contexts where:

- governments have limited fiscal or institutional capacity
- formal strategies may be patchy or under-documented
- yet communities, local administrators, and certain sectors have developed **robust informal and hybrid systems** for coping with recurrent shocks

Examples include:

- local grain storage and rotational savings groups in parts of East and West Africa
- informal cross-border trade networks in West Africa and Central America that keep food and fuel flowing when formal routes are disrupted

- community-managed water and forest systems in parts of Asia and Latin America, which provide buffers against climate extremes

These practices are not neatly codified into laws or glossy strategies. They often coexist uneasily with formal policy, and can be undermined by poorly designed reforms.

For RTT, silent resilience raises three important questions:

1. **How do we recognise and protect it?**

   External actors (including well-meaning donors) sometimes disrupt local systems in the name of formalisation, efficiency, or modernisation, inadvertently weakening resilience.

2. **How do we connect it to national and regional frameworks?**

   Silent resilience can provide local buffers but may lack scale. The challenge is to integrate it into broader preparedness without suffocating it.

3. **How do we avoid romanticising it?**

   Informal resilience often rests on unpaid labour, social obligation, and unequal power dynamics. It is not a substitute for state responsibility, but it can be a starting point.

RTT's value here is conceptual: it offers a vocabulary to **bring these practices into policy conversations**, not as curiosities but as components of a broader resilience strategy that includes, rather than erases, local knowledge.

9. Cross-Cutting Lessons

Looking across these regional models, a few patterns emerge.

1. **There is no single RTT template.**

   The EU leverages scale and legal frameworks; Taiwan concentrates high-tech capacity; Finland builds institutions and social norms; the UAE invests state capital in technological fixes; Vietnam rides trade integration while feeling for resilience footholds; Brazil uses its resource base to build energy and food security. They are all, in different ways, working with pieces of RTT.

2. **Resilience is rarely declared; it is layered.**

   Most of what looks RTT-like today emerged from previous concerns, war memories in Finland, energy crises in Brazil, food import dependence in the UAE, industrial ambition in Taiwan and Vietnam, integration priorities in the EU. RTT does not ask countries to start from zero. It asks them to **organise what they already have** around a clearer strategic logic.

3. **Governance is the differentiator.**

   The biggest differences are not about whether a country has stockpiles or industrial policy, but about how they are governed: transparent or opaque, cooperative or top-down, reviewed or static.

4. **Justice keeps returning as a structural issue.**

   In every case, questions of inclusion, regional balance, labour conditions, and global equity matter. Resilience built on growing internal or external inequality will be brittle.

10. Toolkit: Using Regional Models Without Copying Them

For policymakers and researchers thinking about RTT in their own context, these examples can be useful, as long as they are treated as **sources of insight, not templates.**

Toolkit 13 - Learning from Regional RTT Models

1. **Identify analogues.**

   Which case shares elements of your situation? Are you more like Finland (small, high trust, institutionally dense), Vietnam (trade-dependent, upgrading), Brazil (resource-rich), or the UAE (import-dependent, capital-rich)?

2. **Map transferable elements.**

   From that analogue, list practices that might translate, e.g., Finland's security-of-supply pools, Taiwan's industrial-policy discipline, the EU's vulnerability mapping, Brazil's biofuel strategy, the UAE's food governance.

3. **Stress-test against your constraints.**

   Ask: what would break if we tried this here? Do we have the legal, fiscal, and social infrastructure to sustain it? What would we need to build first?

4. **Engage "silent resilience."**

   Identify local practices in your own country that already perform resilience functions. Map how they might complement more formal RTT-style measures.

5. **Avoid cargo-cult policies.**

   Do not build a NESA because Finland has one, or a chip act because Taiwan does. Start from your actual essential sectors and vulnerabilities, and design institutions accordingly.

6. **Embed equity from the start.**

   Each example shows that who benefits and who carries the cost matters. Use regional experiences to anticipate where inequality might undermine your own efforts.

11. Conclusion: Many Paths, One Underlying Question

In every region examined in this chapter, the same underlying question appears, even if it is phrased differently:

What must we be able to count on, in ourselves and in our partners, when the world turns turbulent?

The European Union answers with open strategic autonomy. Taiwan answers with a silicon shield. Finland answers with stockpiles, institutions, and social habits. The UAE answers with technology-driven food security. Vietnam answers with adaptive integration. Brazil answers with fuel and food redundancy. Many Global South communities answer with quiet, everyday systems that rarely make news.

Resilient Trade Theory does not ask them to converge on a single model. It simply invites them to see their efforts as part of a shared project: **designing interdependence and domestic capacity so that shocks do not become catastrophes, and coercion does not become destiny**.

The next chapters zoom back out to that shared project, asking how RTT should evolve in a world of polycrisis, and what it demands from leaders who must govern not only for comfort today, but for continuity in the storms ahead.

Endnotes

1. European Commission Joint Research Centre. (2025). *Open Strategic Autonomy: Concepts, Metrics and Policy Implications.*
2. European Parliament Research Service. (2023). *Europe's open strategic autonomy: Building resilience while preserving openness.*
3. Liu, R. C., Tang, H.W., Kao, Y.C., Chou, Y.T. (2025). From vulnerabilities to resilience: Taiwan's semiconductor industry and geopolitical challenges. *Telecommuncations Policy. 49|(1).*
4. Liu, J., & Ekman, A. (2024). *From domination to co-creation: How Taiwan sustains semiconductor leadership through adaptive industrial policy.* Institute for Security & Development Policy.
5. Center for Strategic and International Studies. (2025). *Silicon Island: Assessing Taiwan's importance to U.S. economic growth and security.*
6. Huoltovarmuuskeskus (National Emergency Supply Agency). (2024). *Strategy for 2024–2027.*
7. Nordic Labour Journal. (2025, August 28). *Finnish preparedness – a model for the Nordic region.*
8. UAE Government. (2024). *National Food Security Strategy 2051* (updated brief).
9. AGSI. (2024). *The UAE's path to food self-sufficiency: Innovation, investment, and resilience.*
10. World Bank. (2024). *Viet Nam 2045: Trading up in a changing world.*
11. Vietnam Law & Legal Forum. (2025, October 3). Collaborative efforts needed to boost Viet Nam's supply chain growth.

12. IRENA & TEC. (2025). *Brazil's biofuel industry: Policy, markets, and resilience.*

13. Mercure, J.-F., et al. (2019). System complexity and policy integration challenges: The Brazilian energy-agriculture-water nexus. *Renewable and Sustainable Energy Reviews, 105,* 230–243.

CHAPTER 14

RESILIENCE IN A POLYCRISIS WORLD

Resilient Trade Theory (RTT) was born from a simple intuition: in a turbulent world, nations and blocs must know what they *cannot afford* to lose, and organise trade around that reality. Up to now, we have mostly treated shocks one at a time, pandemics, wars, financial crises, cyberattacks, climate events.

But we do not live in a "one shock at a time" world. We live in what many now call a **polycrisis**: a condition in which crises in multiple systems overlap, interact, and amplify one another in ways that are more damaging than the sum of their parts.

In this setting, resilience is not just about having spare capacity or extra stock. It is about navigating **entangled risks**:

- climate disruption damaging harvests and ports while also raising food prices and fuelling political anger
- artificial intelligence (AI) simultaneously enabling better risk management and introducing new systemic vulnerabilities
- demographic shifts reshaping labour markets, fiscal balances, and the social contract in ways that make adaptation harder or, in some cases, easier

This chapter asks what RTT looks like in that kind of world.

It does three things:

1. It sketches how RTT must adapt to three structural forces: **climate disruption, AI risk, and demographic change**.
2. It frames RTT as an **evolving policy doctrine**, not a static blueprint.
3. It reflects on the **new balance between economic interdependence and national autonomy** in an age where shocks travel quickly and compound deeply.

The aim is not to offer final answers. It is to show how RTT can remain useful when the ground beneath it is moving.

1. The Polycrisis Frame

"Polycrisis" is not just a dramatic word. It describes a specific pattern: crises in multiple global systems, financial, ecological, technological, geopolitical, becoming **causally entangled**, producing harms greater than the sum of their parts.

In practice, this means:

- **Timing coincidence** - shocks arriving together or in quick succession.
- **Feedback loops** - a climate event triggers supply chain disruptions, which feed inflation, which fuels political polarisation, which weakens the capacity to respond to the next shock.
- **Cross-domain dependencies** - digital systems reliant on fragile energy grids, health systems reliant on just-in-time pharmaceuticals, financial systems reliant on opaque AI tools.

For trade and economic policy, the polycrisis frame does two important things:

- It breaks the habit of thinking in **single-issue silos** (for example, trade vs. climate vs. technology).
- It forces us to treat some shocks not as outliers, but as **baseline conditions**.

RTT was already designed with systemic risk in mind. But the polycrisis lens pushes it further. It suggests that resilience measures cannot be optimised for one threat in isolation; they must be robust across multiple, interacting hazards. That is a higher bar, and a different kind of design challenge.

2. Climate Disruption: From External Risk to Structural Parameter

Climate change is no longer a distant "risk factor." It is a **structural feature** of the world economy. The evidence is everywhere:

- Rising frequency and severity of extreme weather events disrupting ports, transport corridors, and industrial clusters.
- "Climateflation" - climate-driven shocks pushing up food and input prices, with disproportionate impacts on low-income households.
- Projections that agrifood systems will face significant yield declines in many regions, while being responsible for a large share of global emissions.

For RTT, this means three shifts.

2.1 Climate as a Driver of Essentiality

Climate impacts are not evenly distributed across sectors. They fall heavily on:

- **Agriculture and food** - droughts, floods, heatwaves, pest outbreaks.
- **Energy systems** - hydropower variability, cooling water constraints for thermal plants, damage to transmission.
- **Transport and logistics** - flooded ports, heat-damaged rail, low river levels disrupting barge traffic.
- **Digital infrastructure** - data centres and cables exposed to storms, fires, and heat.

These are all Tier 1 or Tier 2 sectors in RTT terms. Climate disruption therefore *reinforces* their essentiality and adds a new dimension: we are not only protecting them from geopolitical coercion, but from **physical instability**.

In practice, this means:

- when mapping vulnerabilities, climate exposure must be treated as a core variable, not an add-on
- when classifying goods, climate-sensitive inputs (seeds, fertilisers, water treatment chemicals, grid components) deserve special attention

2.2 Climate-Resilient Capacity, not just Capacity

RTT's emphasis on domestic and allied capacity in essentials must now become **climate-resilient capacity.**

For example:

- Food security strategies cannot simply assume historical climate patterns; they must account for shifting agro-ecological zones, water constraints, and the risk of simultaneous crop failures in multiple breadbaskets.
- Energy resilience cannot rest solely on fossil reserves if those reserves are vulnerable to climate policies, or if

physical infrastructure (pipelines, refineries, coastal LNG terminals) is at risk from storms and sea-level rise.

- Supply chain strategies must consider that some key nodes may face **chronic stress**, not just occasional disruption.

UNDP and others now talk explicitly about **climate-resilient, net-zero supply chains**, particularly in agrifood systems where both mitigation and adaptation stakes are high. RTT is a natural partner to that agenda: it already cares about where things are produced, how dependent we are on single nodes, and what happens in crisis.

2.3 Climate-Aware Trade Design

Climate also affects how we design trade:

- **Diversified sourcing** cannot just be about politics; it must also be about climate exposure. Two suppliers in different countries may still share the same river basin or climate regime; that is not real diversification.
- **Resilience clauses** in trade agreements can explicitly reference climate shocks, establishing protocols for export restrictions, mutual support, and critical corridor protection when climate events hit multiple parties at once.
- **Carbon and climate policies** (for example, border adjustments, green industrial strategies) must be designed to avoid inadvertently undermining resilience in low-income, climate-vulnerable countries that supply essentials.

In a polycrisis world, climate is not a separate policy area. It is the stage on which the entire resilience drama unfolds.

3. Artificial Intelligence: Tool, Threat, and Terrain

Artificial intelligence brings a different kind of complexity. On one hand, AI can help:

- model supply chain risks
- optimise logistics
- detect anomalies in critical infrastructure
- support early warning systems

On the other hand, AI introduces **systemic risks** of its own:

- AI systems embedded in finance, energy, and logistics can create opaque, tightly coupled processes prone to sudden failure.
- Concentration of AI capabilities, compute, data, foundational models, in a few firms and countries generates new forms of dependency and potential coercion.
- Generative AI can amplify disinformation, undermine trust in institutions, and destabilise democratic decision-making at precisely the moment when calm coordination is needed.

RTT needs to treat AI in three overlapping roles: **infrastructure, amplifier, and arena.**

3.1 AI as Critical Infrastructure

As high-capability AI systems become embedded in payment systems, logistics platforms, grid management, and industrial control, they start to look like **Tier 1 enabling infrastructure**.

That raises RTT-style questions:

- Who controls the underlying models and platforms?
- Where is the compute physically located, and under which jurisdiction?
- How concentrated is chip production, cloud capacity, and model development?

We already know, for example, that advanced AI chips are heavily concentrated in a few companies and geographies, many of them tied to the same geopolitical fault lines that worry strategists in other domains.

RTT's response is straightforward in principle:

- treat AI-related hardware and core model infrastructure in much the same way we treat other critical digital assets
- avoid single points of failure in chips, data centres, and foundational models
- push for **diversified, allied production** of key AI components, including chips and secure cloud capacity, particularly for essential public functions

3.2 AI as Risk Amplifier

Even when AI is not itself an essential good, it can magnify risks elsewhere:

- high-speed, opaque trading algorithms can destabilise financial markets
- deepfakes and targeted disinformation can erode social cohesion, a crucial resilience asset we explored in Chapter 10
- automated decision systems can generate systemic bias in access to credit, insurance, or social services, undermining confidence in institutions

RTT cannot solve these problems alone, but it can insist that **resilience governance** includes AI-specific stress tests:

- What happens to essential systems if key AI providers fail, are compromised, or withdraw service?
- Are there manual or alternative pathways to keep core functions running if AI-driven automation breaks down?
- Do our resilience simulations include AI-related failure modes (for example, simultaneous model errors across multiple sectors)?

3.3 AI as Arena for Global Justice

Finally, AI is a test case for **global distribution of opportunity and risk.** WTO modelling suggests that AI could significantly increase global trade, but with disproportionate gains for high-income economies unless infrastructure and skills gaps are reduced.

From an RTT perspective:

- if AI becomes another domain where a few actors control essential capacities, we will have created a new layer of trade and security dependency
- if low- and middle-income countries are locked out of AI benefits, the legitimacy of any resilience order that claims to be fair will erode

RTT therefore sits naturally alongside calls for **inclusive AI governance**: wider access to compute, data, and models; safeguards against monopolistic control; and global bodies with enough authority to monitor systemic AI risks and coordinate responses.

In summary: AI is not just another sector. It is a cross-cutting force that reshapes how resilience is built, and how it fails.

4. Demographic Shifts: Ageing, Youth, and Labour for Resilience

Demography may be quieter than climate or AI, but it is no less structural. Many advanced and middle-income economies are ageing rapidly; some lower-income regions still have young, growing populations. Both patterns affect resilience.

4.1 Ageing Societies and Resilience Capacity

Ageing brings several challenges:

- shrinking working-age populations can limit the supply of labour in essential sectors (healthcare, energy, logistics, agriculture)
- fiscal pressures, pensions, healthcare, constrain the resources available for resilience investments
- political focus may tilt toward short-term consumption and status-quo protection rather than long-term adaptation

OECD and other analyses suggest that without policy change, ageing will drag down growth and strain intergenerational fairness, particularly in countries like Japan, Italy, and South Korea.

From an RTT standpoint, this raises practical questions:

- Who will work in essential sectors in 20–30 years?
- How do we design **labour systems and migration policies** that sustain resilience without overburdening younger generations?
- How do we ensure that resilience measures themselves (for example, care infrastructure, energy transition jobs) are used to **renew the social contract**, not deepen age-based tension?

Emerging work on ageing and resilience shows that policy choices matter: countries that invest in lifelong learning, flexible work, and inclusive financial systems can maintain or even improve resilience despite ageing.

4.2 Young Societies and Resilience Opportunity

On the other side, many countries with young populations face:

- high underemployment and informality
- pressure on education, housing, and basic services
- vulnerability to migration pressures and political volatility if expectations are unmet

For RTT, these are **potential resilience assets**, if harnessed. Young societies can:

- staff essential sectors if offered decent work and training
- supply the skills needed for green and digital transitions
- innovate local resilience solutions if given space and support

The risk is that climate, debt, and trade shocks undermine these possibilities, turning demographic advantage into instability. Here, RTT's emphasis on **equity, domestic capacity, and international justice** becomes intergenerational: resilience strategies must avoid loading young populations, at home or abroad, with the costs of past inaction.

4.3 Migration as Resilience Policy

Demographic imbalances make migration an unavoidable part of resilience planning:

- Ageing countries may require migrant labour to staff essential sector.

- Climate-affected regions may see rising outbound migration regardless of policy preferences.
- Trade and investment decisions will intersect with patterns of people movement.

RTT does not dictate migration policy. It simply recognises that **labour supply, skills, and mobility** are as important to resilient trade as ports and factories. Any realistic doctrine for the polycrisis era must integrate demographic trends into its understanding of strategic capacity.

5. RTT as an Evolving Doctrine

Climate disruption, AI, and demographic change are not separate "add-ons" to RTT. They are examples of a deeper truth: **RTT is not a fixed program.** It is a doctrine that must evolve as the structure of global risk evolves.

What does it mean for a policy doctrine to evolve?

5.1 From Snapshot to Process

RTT began with a conceptual snapshot:

- classify sectors
- build capacity
- design differentiated trade
- anchor in social cohesion and ethical duty

In a polycrisis world, that snapshot must become a **continuous process**:

- classification lists updated as technologies and threats change (for example, AI infrastructure moving from Tier 3 to Tier 1 over a decade)
- capacity plans revised as climate projections sharpen and demographic realities unfold

- trade agreements amended to include new resilience clauses
- governance bodies (like a Resilience Trade Authority) mandated to horizon-scan across domains

In other words, RTT becomes less like a blueprint and more like a **living operating system**: stable in its core values, but updated regularly in its applications.

5.2 Feedback from Practice

The cases in the previous chapter, EU, Taiwan, Finland, UAE, Vietnam, Brazil, and "silent resilience" practices, illustrate that RTT-like ideas will be tested in very different conditions. Some will work; some will fail; some will have unintended consequences.

An honest doctrine:

- **learns from experiments** (including its own missteps)
- incorporates new evidence (for example, about how much diversification actually improves resilience, or how climate impacts materialise in specific supply chains)
- adjusts its tools accordingly, without abandoning its basic commitments to security, equity, and openness where safe

5.3 Normative Core, Adaptive Shell

To remain coherent, RTT must distinguish between:

- a **normative core** - obligations to protect populations, secure essentials, treat workers with dignity, and engage the world without naivety
- an **adaptive shell** - sector lists, partner choices, specific instruments, and institutional designs that change over time

In the polycrisis era, doctrines that claim to offer permanent answers will not survive contact with reality. Doctrines that provide a durable direction while respecting complexity have a chance.

RTT aspires to the latter: **steady in purpose, flexible in practice.**

6. A New Balance: Interdependence and Autonomy in the Polycrisis Era

Finally, we return to a question that has shadowed this entire book: How should countries and blocs balance **economic interdependence** with **national autonomy**?

In an age of polycrisis, the old answers, "more trade equals more peace" on one side, "self-sufficiency at any cost" on the other, look increasingly inadequate.

6.1 What Autonomy Is, and Isn't

Autonomy in RTT is not isolation. It is the **ability to make consequential decisions under pressure** without being forced into submission by external leverage.

That requires:

- domestic or allied capacity in essentials
- diversified and trusted relationships in key dependencies
- internal social cohesion strong enough to withstand shocks

It does *not* require:

- producing everything at home
- cutting ties with adversaries in all domains
- retreating into small markets and stagnant technology pools

6.2 What Interdependence Is, and Isn't

Interdependence, in RTT's view, is not blind openness. It is a pattern of **mutual exposure and mutual benefit** that:

- lowers costs and increases opportunity in non-essential sectors
- spreads innovation
- supports collective problem-solving in domains like climate and health

It does *not* mean:

- accepting concentrated dependencies in essentials
- tolerating coercive practices as the price of access
- treating all partners as equally reliable regardless of governance, behaviour, or crisis record

6.3 The Balance Point

In a polycrisis world, the balance looks roughly like this:

- **High autonomy in essentials**, achieved through domestic capacity plus allied interdependence.
- **High interdependence in non-essentials**, maintained through open trade, investment, and knowledge flows.
- **Shared governance of systemic risks**, climate, AI, pandemics, cyber, and financial stability treated as common concerns requiring cooperative frameworks.

That balance will be contested. Different societies will draw the line in different places. The role of RTT is not to fix the balance once and for all, but to **clarify the trade-offs** and provide tools to manage them.

7. Toolkit: Stress-Testing RTT for the Polycrisis Era

To make these ideas concrete, it helps to ask a few hard questions of any resilience strategy.

Toolkit 14 - Polycrisis Checks for RTT

1. **Climate stress test.**

   For each essential sector, ask: how will plausible climate scenarios affect production, logistics, and trade? What happens if two or three climate-exposed nodes fail at once?

2. **AI dependency map.**

   List where AI is embedded in essential systems. Who controls the models and compute? What are the fallback options if they fail or are withdrawn?

3. **Demographic horizon scan.**

   Project labour needs in essential sectors over 10-30 years under your demographic path. What mix of training, technology, and migration will sustain capacity?

4. **Compound scenario exercise.**

   Design at least one exercise that combines shocks, for example, a climate event that disrupts ports, an AI-related outage in logistics software, and a domestic political crisis. Can your institutions cope?

5. **Equity and justice review.**

   Identify who bears the cost of your resilience measures, by class, region, generation, and internationally. Are you exporting vulnerability, or sharing burdens fairly?

6. **Doctrinal update rhythm.**

   Establish a cycle (for example, every three to five years) in which essential lists, alliance structures, and trade instruments are reviewed explicitly in light of new risks and evidence.

These are not boxes to be ticked and forgotten. They are prompts for ongoing reflection in a world where the risk landscape is not static.

8. Conclusion: Living with Depth, Not Just with Speed

The polycrisis era is often described in terms of speed: faster shocks, faster information, faster contagion. RTT, as adapted in this chapter, adds another word: **depth**.

Resilience in this world is about:

- depth of capacity in essentials
- depth of trust within societies
- depth of alliances that share more than slogans
- depth of reflection in doctrines that do not pretend the world is simpler than it is

Climate disruption, AI risk, and demographic shifts ensure that the 21st century will not offer long stretches of calm. The question is not whether turbulence will come. It is whether nations and blocs will have built systems and relationships capable of withstanding it, without abandoning openness, justice, or self-respect.

Resilient Trade Theory cannot promise safety. It can offer a way to think and act that treats safety not as an accident, but as a responsibility. In a polycrisis world, that is as close to certainty as we are likely to get.

Endnotes

1. Lawrence, M., Janzwood, S., & Homer-Dixon, T. (2024). Global polycrisis: The causal mechanisms of crisis entanglement. *Global Sustainability, 7*, e10.
2. World Economic Forum. (2023). *Global Risks Report 2023*; Torkington, S. (2023, January 13). We're on the brink of a polycrisis. How worried should we be? World Economic Forum.
3. Economist Impact. (2024). Climate change's disruptive impact on global supply chains; BCI. (2024). *Supply Chain Resilience Report 2024*; Earth-Scan. (2024). How climate change is impacting your supply chain.
4. Autonomy. (2025). *Climateflation* report; The Guardian. (2025, July 28). 'Climateflation' could push up UK food prices by more than a third by 2050.
5. UNDP. (2025). *Pathways to climate-resilient net zero supply chains.*
6. Narayan, N. (2025). The impact of climate change on supply chain management. *Journal of Climate and Business Analytics.*
7. Daníelsson, J., et al. (2022). Artificial intelligence and systemic risk. *Journal of Banking & Finance, 142*, 106505.
8. Ilčić, A. (2025). Artificial intelligence, complexity, and systemic resilience in global governance. *Frontiers in Artificial Intelligence.*
9. European Stability Mechanism. (2025, July 29). Preparing for systemic risks in the age of generative artificial intelligence (blog).
10. Oxford Insights. (2025, April 3). Systemic AI risk is slipping off the international agenda. Should we care?

11. NAVEX. (2025, August 7). Exactly what are 'systemic' AI risks, anyway?
12. WTO. (2025). *The future of trade: AI, inequality, and inclusive opportunities* (press coverage in Financial Times, October 2025).
13. Times of India. (2025, October). Concentration of AI capabilities poses systemic risks: NPCI chairman.
14. Sibylline. (2025). *A looming global polycrisis: China, Taiwan, and AI* (summary reported by MarketWatch).
15. Global Governance Centre. (2024). UN Summit of the Future: A critical moment for global AI governance.
16. OECD. (2025). *Employment Outlook 2025: Demographic change, economic growth, and intergenerational inequalities*; McKinsey Global Institute. (2025). *Dependency and depopulation: Confronting the consequences of a new demographic reality*; OECD/World Economic Forum. (2025). *Economic resilience in ageing societies.*
17. UNDRR. (2025). *Critical responses to global systemic risk in an era of polycrisis*; Global Platform for Disaster Risk Reduction. (2025). Understanding systemic risk in the age of polycrisis (session TS1-1).

PART V

Conclusion

CHAPTER 15

RESILIENCE AS A STRATEGIC VIRTUE

Resilient Trade Theory (RTT) began with a deceptively simple question:

What must a country or bloc be able to count on when everything around it becomes uncertain?

Over the previous chapters, that question has unfolded into a full framework: a way of thinking about trade, capacity, labour, governance, diplomacy, and justice under conditions that are no longer stable or predictable.

This final chapter steps back. It is less about additional tools and more about **meaning**. What does it actually mean to treat resilience not as a technical add-on, but as a strategic virtue, something we choose to value in its own right, not just as a side effect of growth?

And if we do that, what does it demand from:

- how we judge economic success
- how we design institutions and alliances
- and how leaders, political, economic, and civic, understand their responsibilities

The underlying claim of this book is straightforward:

Resilient trade is not a temporary response to a rough patch. It is a new baseline for strategic thinking in a century defined by systemic risk.

The rest of this chapter unpacks that claim and sketches what it asks of those who will have to make choices in its shadow.

1. From "Peace Through Trade" to "Strength Through Balance"

For much of the post-war era, the dominant story ran like this:

- Liberalise trade.
- Integrate economies.
- Let comparative advantage and global supply chains do their work.

If all went well, the result would be higher incomes, cheaper goods, and, not incidentally, a more peaceful world, as states became too intertwined to fight.[1]

There was truth in that story. Trade has lifted hundreds of millions out of poverty. Integration has given many countries access to technologies and markets that would otherwise have been unreachable. Even now, much of the global South still sees trade as a central route to development, and rightly so.

But the last two decades have revealed the **blind spots** in the "peace through trade" paradigm:

- It assumed shocks would be local and occasional, not global and overlapping.
- It treated power, coercion, and strategic rivalry as side issues, not as forces that could be channelled through trade itself.[2]

- It focused on efficiency in normal times, not on continuity under strain.

When pandemics close factories on three continents at once, when extreme weather hits multiple breadbaskets in the same season, when key technologies are used as geopolitical leverage, the promise that "more trade equals more stability" looks fragile.[3]

None of this means trade has failed. It means the old assumption that openness alone would deliver peace and prosperity needs to be **replaced with something more honest**:

Not peace through trade at any cost, but strength through balance, a balance between openness and autonomy, efficiency and redundancy, interdependence and strategic control.

RTT is an attempt to give that balance a vocabulary and a structure.

2. What It Means to Call Resilience a Virtue

We have treated resilience as a goal throughout this book. But calling it a **virtue** does something additional. Virtues are:

- not just instrumental, they have **moral weight**
- not just individual traits, they can be embedded in institutions and systems
- not just responses to crises, they shape how we act long before the crisis arrives

Prudence, for example, is a classic strategic virtue: the ability to act with foresight and proportion, rather than impulse. Courage is another: the willingness to act in defence of something valuable, despite risk.

Resilience sits alongside these. It is:

- the capacity to **endure without breaking**
- the ability to **adapt without losing core identity or values**
- the discipline to **build margin and redundancy** even when the pressure is to cut costs to the bone

When we say "resilience is a strategic virtue," we are saying:

- it deserves to be **weighted explicitly** in decisions, not left as an afterthought
- trading a small amount of average-case efficiency for a large increase in worst-case endurance can be an **ethically and strategically superior choice**
- governments have a duty not only to maximise output, but to **protect continuity of life and dignity** under foreseeable strain[4]

Virtues also imply **character**. A resilient trade system is not simply one with more warehouses or more factories. It is one in which:

- short-term gains do not automatically overrule long-term security
- leaders are willing to say "no" to attractive but dangerous dependencies
- societies accept that some redundancy and some local capacity are not waste, but insurance

That is a cultural shift as much as a policy shift.

3. Redefining What Counts as "Success"

If resilience is a virtue, we have to ask a blunt question:

How would we know if our trade and economic systems were actually resilient, not just prosperous?

Traditional metrics, GDP growth, export volumes, investment flows, tell us important things. They do **not** tell us:

- how quickly a food system recovers from a failed harvest
- whether a country can manufacture basic medicines if imports stop
- how dependent a grid is on a single foreign supplier of spare parts
- whether essential workers can afford to stay in their roles
- how deeply trust in institutions runs when hard trade-offs are needed

In a resilience frame, **success looks different**. It includes questions like:

- Can we keep food, energy, and health systems functioning through severe shocks?
- Are our dependencies in essentials **diversified and politically stable**?
- Do essential workers receive a **liveable wage and meaningful voice**, or are they treated as expendable?
- Are there **governance bodies**, like a Resilient Trade Authority, that can coordinate response without improvising every time?

- Do our trade agreements include **continuity and cooperation clauses**, or only tariff schedules?
- Can we adapt our policies as climate, technology, and demographics shift, without having to tear everything up each time?

None of this means abandoning growth or trade volumes as metrics. It means **adding a resilience layer**:

- new indicators that track concentration in essentials, stock levels, response times
- social indicators that track trust, cohesion, and perceived fairness[5]
- international indicators that reflect how our choices affect vulnerabilities in other countries, not only our own

A system that scores high on growth but low on continuity and justice is not, in RTT's terms, a success. It is a system borrowing stability from the future.

4. The Core Architecture of RTT, In One View

By now, the key pieces of RTT should feel familiar, but it is helpful to gather them in one place.

1. Essential vs Non-essential Sectors

We separate goods and services into tiers:

- Tier 1: lifeline sectors (food staples, basic medicines, core energy, water treatment, critical digital and logistics infrastructure).
- Tier 2: enabling sectors (specialised inputs, logistics nodes, grid components).
- Tier 3-4: important but non-essential and discretionary sectors.

This classification is revisited regularly and used to **prioritise** attention, investment, and protection.

2. Strategic Capacity in Essentials

For Tier 1 and key Tier 2 sectors, we:

- maintain meaningful domestic or allied production and stockpiles
- treat resilience as a guiding test for public investment
- design infrastructure and supply chains to be robust, not just cheap

3. Labour Systems as Resilience Assets

We treat workers in essentials, agriculture, energy, logistics, health, defence-relevant production, as central to resilience:

- a **minimum liveable wage** as a baseline, not a luxury
- vocational and higher education aligned with strategic needs
- regional rebalancing, so resilience jobs strengthen cohesion rather than deepen divides[6]

4. Governance and Oversight

We establish institutions with the authority and remit to:

- map vulnerabilities
- audit resilience
- run simulations
- coordinate cross-ministerial and public-private action

And we ensure these institutions are **transparent and revisable**, not partisan tools.

5. Differentiated Trade Policy

We reject all-or-nothing trade ideology:

- in essentials, we use selective protection, friend-shoring, and continuity clauses
- in non-essentials, we keep borders **as open as possible**
- we embed resilience and equity into trade agreements, not only market access

6. Social Cohesion as Infrastructure

We understand that none of the above will work if:

- large regions feel abandoned
- essential workers are precarious
- communities see resilience policies as imposed rather than shared

So we link resilience investments to **cooperative ownership, SMEs, and community wealth**, and we use **inclusive planning** to build consent.

7. Diplomacy and Global Justice

We recognise that national resilience is interwoven with global stability:

- we build **resilience alliances** rather than isolated fortresses
- we support pacts on pandemics, climate, and cyber that share capacity and access
- we treat justice, especially for vulnerable states and younger generations, as a **stability condition**, not an optional extra.[7]

Taken together, these elements define what "strength through balance" looks like in practice.

5. What the Future Demands From Trade and Policy

If we take RTT seriously, trade and economic policy in the coming decades will have to carry **more weight** than in the past. It will be asked to deliver:

- growth and innovation
- resilience in essentials
- reduced exposure to coercion
- contributions to climate and ecological goals
- and a meaningful role in rebuilding social cohesion

That is a demanding brief. It implies several shifts.

5.1 From Single-Objective to Multi-Objective Design

Policies built for a simpler era often maximised a single variable, usually efficiency or growth, under the assumption that other goals would follow. RTT requires multi-objective design:

- trade agreements that balance access, resilience, and equity
- industrial policies that balance innovation, environmental limits, and strategic sufficiency
- labour policies that balance competitiveness, dignity, and regional balance

This does not mean paralysis. It means **being explicit** about trade-offs and choosing in full view, rather than letting one objective quietly dominate.

5.2 From Reactive Crisis Management to Continuous Preparedness

If the last twenty years taught us anything, it is that ad hoc crisis management is not enough. RTT envisions:

- regular stress-tests for supply chains and essential infrastructure
- standing crisis coordination mechanisms with clear triggers
- budgets that include steady investment in resilience, not only emergency supplements

Preparedness becomes a **permanent function**, not a temporary task after each disaster.

5.3 From "Export of Vulnerabilities" to Shared Responsibility

Traditional trade narratives rarely asked how one country's policies affected the resilience of others. RTT insists that:

- hoarding essentials in crisis, at the expense of weaker countries, is not only ethically troubling; it undermines long-term stability
- closing off key technologies or minerals without pathways for inclusive access can fuel resentment and realignment
- building resilience **with** others, through shared stockpiles, co-produced capacity, fair technology access, is more durable than building it against them[8]

In short: the future of trade is not only about goods and services; it is about **how risk and responsibility are distributed**.

6. What the Future Demands From Leadership

Frameworks do not implement themselves. They are carried, or dropped, by people.

RTT, if taken seriously, asks something quite specific from leadership in governments, firms, and institutions.

6.1 The Courage to Say "Enough"

Leaders will need the courage to:

- say "no" to arrangements that are cheap today but dangerous tomorrow
- acknowledge that some short-term growth will be sacrificed for long-term continuity
- resist pressure from interests that want "strategic" labels without genuine essentiality

That means being willing to take political heat in the present to prevent avoidable harm in the future. It is not easy work.

6.2 The Discipline to Think in Systems

Resilience cannot be managed in silos. Leaders, political, bureaucratic, corporate, will need the capacity to see:

- how decisions in energy affect food, and vice versa
- how labour markets, education, and regional policy shape resilience
- how trade decisions echo through social cohesion and international alliances

This is partly a skills question (systems thinking, risk literacy), and partly an organisational one (whether institutions make cross-sector work possible).

6.3 The Honesty to Speak in Plain Language

RTT also requires leaders to **talk differently** to their publics:

- to explain why some sectors get special protection and others do not

- to be transparent about vulnerabilities instead of hiding them
- to make the case that resilience costs something, money, convenience, sometimes choice, and that those costs are worth bearing

People are more capable of understanding complex trade-offs than they are often given credit for. What they resent is being misled or reassured falsely.

6.4 The Humility to Cooperate

No country, bloc, or firm can do this alone. Leadership in an RTT era includes:

- forming alliances without seeking domination
- participating seriously in global risk governance, even when it constrains unilateral freedom
- listening to smaller or poorer partners when designing resilience frameworks that will affect them

Humility is not a word often used in strategic discussions. Yet in a world of shared vulnerabilities, it may be one of the most practical virtues available.

7. Questions to Carry Forward

Ending a book like this with a list of prescriptions would be misleading. RTT is a beginning, not a finished doctrine. So instead of more instructions, it may be more honest to close with questions, the kind leaders, researchers, and citizens will have to keep asking.

Toolkit 15 - Questions for the Next Phase

1. **What are we still assuming is stable that may not be?**

   In our sector maps, trade agreements, and alliances, where are we quietly relying on conditions that could realistically change?

2. **Who benefits from our current vulnerabilities?**

   Which actors, domestic or foreign, gain from the status quo, and how will they resist change?

3. **Where are we over-correcting?**

   Are there areas where "resilience" has become a slogan to justify broad protection or isolation that does little to reduce real risk?

4. **How are young people reading these choices?**

   To those who will live longest with the consequences, do our policies look like stewardship — or like short-termism repackaged?

5. **What would failure look like, and how would we know early?**

   Do we have indicators, forums, and feedback loops that tell us when resilience strategies are drifting off course?

6. **Where can cooperation change our calculus?**

   Are there areas where shared investments or pacts could give us more resilience per unit cost than going alone?

7. **What would it mean, concretely, to be proud of our trade system in 30 years' time?**

   Not just richer, but prouder. What would we need to have preserved, and what would we need to have changed?

These are not rhetorical questions. They are prompts for ongoing work.

8. Closing Reflections: Standing in the Storm

The world ahead will almost certainly be rougher than the one in which the old trade paradigm was built. Climate volatility, geopolitical rivalry, technological upheaval, demographic imbalances, cyber risk, none of these are temporary. They are the weather system in which nations and blocs will now live.

In that environment, hoping that efficiency alone will deliver safety is a kind of wishful thinking. It is not serious enough for the responsibilities we carry.

Resilient Trade Theory does not promise to fix that. It does not promise that carefully designed trade policies and strategic capacity will prevent all crises. They will not. But it does offer something more modest and, perhaps, more valuable:

- a way to **name what must be protected**
- a way to **balance openness with security** without sliding into crude protectionism
- a way to **link economics with ethics**, so that questions of dignity, justice, and intergenerational responsibility are not treated as afterthoughts
- a way to **organise our thinking** so that shocks are anticipated rather than constantly treated as surprises

In the end, the test is simple:

When the storm comes, and it will, will our people still have food, power, medicine, information they can trust, and the freedom to make decisions without external blackmail?

If the answer is "yes, even under strain," then resilience will not just be a word. It will be something real, built in advance, owned collectively.

That is what this book has argued for: not a retreat from the world, but a way of standing in it that is **steadier, more just, and less afraid**. Resilient trade is not a trend. It is a choice about what kind of vulnerability we are willing to live with, and what kind we are no longer willing to accept.

The work of translating that choice into policy and practice now belongs to those who govern, those who produce, and those who hold them to account. RTT is offered as a compass for that journey, not as its destination.

Endnotes

1. Rodrik, D. (2011). *The Globalization Paradox: Democracy and the Future of the World Economy*. W. W. Norton.
2. Baldwin, R. (2016). *The Great Convergence: Information Technology and the New Globalization*. Harvard University Press.
3. World Trade Organization. (2021). *World Trade Report 2021: Economic resilience and trade*. WTO.
4. Jonas, H. (1984). *The Imperative of Responsibility: In Search of an Ethics for the Technological Age*. University of Chicago Press.
5. Aldrich, D. P. (2012). *Building Resilience: Social Capital in Post-Disaster Recovery*. University of Chicago Press.
6. International Labour Organization. (2021). *World Social Protection Report 2020–22: Social protection at the crossroads*. ILO.
7. International Monetary Fund. (2023). *Geo-Economic Fragmentation and the Future of Multilateralism*. IMF.
8. United Nations Development Programme. (2023). *New Threats to Human Security in the Anthropocene: Demanding greater solidarity*. UNDP.

AUTHOR'S CONCLUDING REMARKS

When I first began sketching the ideas that became Resilient Trade Theory, I wasn't trying to invent a new "doctrine." I was trying to find language for something many people were already feeling but struggling to articulate.

That the way we've organised our economies leaves too many citizens, and too many countries, exposed. That fragility has been normalised. And that we have quietly accepted forms of dependency we would never tolerate if we looked at them in daylight.

This book is my attempt to hold that discomfort still for long enough to do something constructive with it.

I'm very aware that, on paper, frameworks like RTT can look neat and controlled. Real life is not like that. Decisions are made by tired human beings, in crowded rooms, under pressure, with incomplete information and political constraints. Interests pull in different directions. Short-term incentives are almost always louder than long-term responsibilities.

So I do not imagine that any government, bloc, or institution will lift Resilient Trade Theory off the page and implement it as written. Nor should they. Context matters. History matters. Culture matters. And plain old luck still plays its part.

What I do hope is more modest, and in a way, more ambitious.

I hope this framework gives you a clearer way to ask better questions:

- Is this dependency one we're genuinely willing to live with?
- Are we building the capacity we will wish we had, ten or twenty years from now?
- Are we treating essential workers as strategic partners, or as an afterthought?
- Are we using trade to export risk to others, or to share responsibility more fairly?
- When we say "resilience," do we mean something concrete, or just something comforting?

If this book has done its job, you will find yourself a little less satisfied with vague reassurances, a little more impatient with slogans, and a little more equipped to insist on detail: which sectors, whose capacity, what kind of redundancy, at whose expense, and for whose benefit.

I also hope you will remember that resilience is not only a matter of design. It is a matter of character.

The systems we build will reflect what we value:

- If we prize only speed and low cost, we will get brittle abundance.
- If we prize control without justice, we will get fortresses that crack from within.

- If we treat people as instruments, labour, consumers, "human capital", we will find they are not there when we need them most.

But if we choose, deliberately, to value continuity of life over marginal gains, dignity over convenience, and shared security over narrow advantage, our systems will begin to look different. Not perfect. Not shock-proof. But less exposed. Less easily coerced. Less afraid.

You may disagree with parts of what I've proposed. You may have better tools, better models, or better examples to bring into the conversation. Good. This work was never meant to be a final word. It is an invitation, to economists, policymakers, diplomats, farmers, engineers, union leaders, students, to bring their own expertise and lived experience to the question of how we keep our societies standing when the ground shifts.

The storms ahead will not wait for us to agree. They will come whether or not our frameworks are tidy.

But we are not helpless passengers in someone else's system. We still have choices about what we build, what we protect, and what we will no longer trade away.

If, after reading this book, you find yourself pushing a little harder—for more honest risk assessments, for fairer treatment of essential workers, for more thoughtful trade agreements, for resilience that includes your neighbours rather than excluding them—then this project will have been worth the effort.

Thank you for taking the time to walk through it with me.

ABOUT THE AUTHOR

Dr. Kenneth Tuttle Wilhelm is a thinker, writer, educator who works at the intersection of business, ethics, education, and moral thought. His work is driven by a simple, persistent question: how can societies remain open to the world while still protecting the people and systems they are ultimately responsible for?

A child of the Vietnam War era, Kenneth grew up with the evening news as a kind of background soundtrack, images of conflict, fragile ceasefires, and economic upheaval. Those early impressions never really left. Over the decades, he has watched oil shocks, financial crises, regional wars, pandemics, and climate stress roll through economies and communities, leaving patterns that felt uncomfortably familiar: political turmoil, economic fallout, and ordinary people asked to absorb the cost.

It was this long arc of observation, across different countries, systems, and crises, that led him to develop **Resilient Trade Theory** and the **Resilient Trade Model**. His work engages directly with policy professionals, academics, and practitioners who are wrestling with supply chain fragility, economic coercion, and the tension between global integration and national autonomy.

Kenneth's writing is marked by a steady concern for the human consequences of abstract decisions. He insists that discussions of trade and strategy cannot be separated from questions of dignity, social cohesion, and intergenerational responsibility. His work often brings together insights from business, political science, ethical leadership, and moral philosophy, while remaining grounded in plain language and practical examples.

Over the years, he has written on themes of resilience, social contracts, and the ethical responsibilities of leadership in chaotic environments. *Resilient Trade Theory* is his first major book dedicated entirely to a comprehensive economic-strategic framework, aimed at policymakers, scholars, and institutional leaders who sense that "efficiency-first" globalisation is no longer enough, and are searching for a more honest, durable way forward.

www.ingramcontent.com/pod-product-compliance
Lightning Source LLC
LaVergne TN
LVHW100300210926
848480LV00003B/975

9798901366011